Second Print (with additions)

Treasure beyond Measure

MAHARAJ CHARAN SINGH

DEDICATED

to

BELOVED MAHARAJ JI

Sweet and ambrosial are Thy words,
Thou art within all, yet aloof,
My winsome charming Lord;
Not kingdom do I crave,
Nor salvation I covet;
I long only for love
Of Thy lotus feet, my Beloved.

(Adi Granth, p. 534)

— Shanti

Treasure

beyond

Measure

SHANTI SETHI

RADHA SOAMI SATSANG BEAS
PUNJAB INDIA

Published by
S. L. Sondhi, Secretary
Radha Soami Satsang Beas
P. O. Dera Baba Jaimal Singh
Punjab, India

© 1991
Radha Soami Satsang Beas
All Rights Reserved
First Edition—15,000 copies, February 1990
Second Edition, enlarged—40,000 copies, January 1991

Laser Typesetting by:
Fastrak Systems
783, Desh Bandhu Gupta Road
New Delhi-110 005
Phones : 51-8265, 51-9298

Printed by:
India Offset Press
A 1, Mayapuri Ind. Area
New Delhi-64

CONTENTS

PART II

PREFACE TO THE SECOND EDITION

How could we ever have known that *Treasure beyond Measure* was to be the last book to be printed and published during the lifetime of Huzur Maharaj Charan Singh Ji?

Mrs. Shanti Sethi started preparing the book sometime in October or November, 1989, and the first edition of 15,000 copies was made available to the sangat hardly five months later at the Dera book stalls in April, 1990. The book sold out immediately. It had been prepared and put through the press in record time and everyone involved with the project made mention of the sense of urgency that accompanied its preparation. No one, at that time, could possibly imagine the reason for urgency, except, of course, our beloved Master, who knew how the next few months would unfold.

In hindsight, we understand that the publication of this book was closely interwoven with Huzur Maharaj Ji's decision to leave the body at the completion of His Mission, which He did on June 1, 1990. As his successor said in His inaugural address, "Huzur Maharaj Ji chose to make a minor illness an excuse for leaving us to merge back into the source of Love and Light from which He came, thus casting a shadow of gloom over the entire world. Medically, he would have recovered from the illness, but having completed the Divine Mission assigned to Him, He chose to cast off the mortal coil."

Mrs. Shanti Sethi has included substantial additional material in this second edition. She has also given a moving account of the last days of Huzur Maharaj Charan Singh Ji's sojourn in this world and has included the inaugural address of the new Master, surcharged with love and humility, delivered on the occasion of the 'Dastarbandi' ceremony.

The first edition, given to us just weeks before the departure of Huzur Maharaj Ji, by revealing such personal details of His life helped us understand the process of transition from one Master to another, acting in the supreme will. It is our earnest submission that this second edition, like the first, will speak directly to the hearts of the sangat and will provide an endless source of inspiration for right conduct in our lives, that we may each travel steadfastly towards self-realization, towards God-realization, and towards meeting with our Master in His Radiant Form.

We would like to express our gratitude to Mrs. Shanti Sethi for her foresight in noting down all the material which provided the base for this book, and for her loving work of compilation. We must also thank Professor K. S. Narang for his most able and meticulous guidance. We are grateful to Miss Louise Hilger and Professor Janak Raj Puri, who revised the whole book and endeavoured to remove the errors and defects of syntax that were present in the first edition because of its hurried preparation. We must thank Mr. John Davidson for his

contribution, and Shri Thakur Das for his untiring
labour of love in typing the manuscript in the short-
est possible time. Last but not least, we are grateful
to Bruce Becker of U.S.A. who has prepared the
index for the entire book.

Words cannot express our profound gratitude
to Huzur Maharaj Ji who, in His benevolence, chose
to reveal Himself through this book, and to His
Beloved Successor, who took up all the facets of
His Master's work in true humility, love and faith.

S. L. SONDHI
Secretary

Radha Soami Satsang Beas
September, 1990

PREFACE TO THE FIRST EDITION

Treasure beyond Measure is a beautiful collection of events concerning Maharaj Charan Singh Ji, beginning from the early days of his life. They were gleaned at random from his diaries, letters and talks, from accounts provided by his friends, from notes made by the compiler, and are being published in that order.

Besides giving an insight into Maharaj Ji's intense love and devotion for his own Satguru, the book also provides us with a glimpse of his deep love and concern for the sangat, of his profound humility and innate grace, his spirit of tolerance and forbearance, his vision and foresight, his compassion and generosity, his kindness and perception, and above all, his dedication to the task allotted to him by his predecessors and the great pains he has taken to accomplish it, sacrificing his own comfort and well-being.

Shanti Sethi, who has had the benefit of close association with Maharaj Ji for the last thirty-seven years, is well qualified to undertake the venture of compiling this book. We are grateful to her for collecting all the information and amplifying her notes, for showing them to Maharaj Ji and obtaining not only his confirmation of the events narrated, but also his elaboration on the events in this book.

We are grateful to John Davidson who, while maintaining the original simplicity of style and expression, has given the narrative a book form; to T. K. Sethi for his help in preparation of the book; to Barbara Maynord, Sharon Porter and Elizabeth Irwin for typing the manuscript; and to Louise Hilger, R. N. Mehta and his group of sevadars for seeing the book through the press.

We find no words to express our deep gratitude to Maharaj Charan Singh Ji for granting us the permission to publish *Treasure beyond Measure* for the benefit of satsangis the world over.

We are confident that satsangis will enjoy the unadorned beauty of this unique book and find it inspiring and elevating.

S. L. SONDHI
Secretary

Radha Soami Satsang Beas
December, 1989

FOREWORD

Down through the years since I became a satsangi in 1953, I have heard so many beautiful incidents concerning Maharaj Ji's life, from his family members, from old satsangis who had been very close to the Master and from Maharaj Ji's casual talk, as well as from satsangs—especially the English meetings. From these and whatever other sources I could find, I have gathered information and made notes.

Every satsangi always wants to know all about the Master, to learn all the little details of his life. It was this common desire, which we all share, that inspired me to turn these notes into book form, to share with everyone.

With Maharaj Ji's grace, the opportunity came my way when Dr. Joshi asked me to take bed rest due to a heart problem from which I was suffering. This gave me plenty of time to reflect, and I utilized this time in writing and gathering whatever I could to compile it into book form.

While slowly recovering from my heart problem, I was 'fortunate' enough to have tripped, breaking a small bone in my foot! This was a blessing in disguise, for with my foot in plaster and still painful after the plaster was removed, I was unable to move about much for several weeks, thus enabling further progress on the book.

While writing, whenever I wanted anything to be explained, I asked Maharaj Ji directly, which he graciously clarified.

I am thankful for the help provided by Mr. T. K. Sethi and to Barbara Maynord, Sharon Porter and Elizabeth Irwin for typing the manuscript.

In this venture, I am also grateful to Mr. John Davidson for taking my handwritten manuscript and turning it into book form, so that everyone could share these precious treasures concerning the Master.

At the end I express my profound sense of gratitude at the feet of my dear and beloved Huzur Maharaj Ji, which in reality is difficult to express. This whole experience has been an overwhelming, inspiring and elevating one for me, and I trust it would be the same for the readers.

SHANTI SETHI

Dera Baba Jaimal Singh
December, 1989

INTRODUCTION

This collection of treasures, mostly of incidents and happenings, has been brought together from a variety of sources. Many of them have been related by Huzur Maharaj Charan Singh Ji, both in satsang and otherwise. Some have been narrated by the Great Master, a few by the Master's mother and some by other disciples of the Masters.

Without exception, the original events have been told either in English or in the vernacular and translated into English. While editing them to read smoothly, all attempts have been made to retain the mood and flavour of the original. To have taken too much liberty with the original narrative would have robbed them of their charm, beauty and character.

Only a few of the treasures in this collection—notably the letters and speeches—have been recorded verbatim. Others have been reconstituted from notes taken during or after the events were related or happened. However, the Master himself took an active part in their assembly, reading all of them through at least three times during the course of their preparation. We can therefore feel assured of the authenticity of everything between these covers.

While such incidents are always of interest, the real value lies in imbibing their spiritual import—in many cases in observing the saintly character of the

Masters and in attempting to allow their qualities to become manifested in our lives. The Masters are ideal examples for us in the spiritual refashioning of our conduct and way of life.

Though the Masters have invariably called their own Master "Maharaj Ji," to avoid confusion in this text the present Master has been referred to as "Maharaj Ji," Sardar Bahadur Jagat Singh Ji as "Sardar Bahadur Ji," Huzur Maharaj Baba Sawan Singh Ji as "the Great Master" and Maharaj Baba Jaimal Singh Ji as "Babaji."

The beauty and spiritual radiance of all that the Masters say and do is beyond compare. As disciples, we can only watch in love and gratitude a grace we hardly understand poured upon ourselves and a multitude of other souls with a nature and consistency that is beyond all normal human comprehension. Only a Master can really understand a Master.

Some glimpse of this divine outpouring is caught between these pages. May it uplift and inspire the hearts, the minds and the souls of all who read, and are inwardly the recipients of the Master's treasure!

All those involved lay their grateful heads at the feet of the Master, without whom nothing would have happened.

JOHN DAVIDSON

Dera Baba Jaimal Singh
December, 1989

PART I

TREASURE BEYOND MEASURE

One day, in a reminiscent mood, Maharaj Ji recalled his first days at the Dera as a Master, and the Dera administration of those times.

Early days at the Dera

Maharaj Ji came to the Dera as the Master around October-November, 1951. At that time, the Dera administration had become very lax. During Sardar Bahadur Ji's time (1948-51), the reins were virtually held by three old and irrepressibly haughty sevadars.

In the langar, there was hardly any control. The head of the langar found it difficult to enforce any discipline; he was merely a figurehead. Many would take the food to their houses or wherever they were camped. In fact, practically half the population of the two neighbouring villages also followed this practice! After every monthly satsang, half of the langar utensils would be missing. Additionally, there were no arrangements for properly allocating accommodation—the sevadar-in-charge could allot or deny, at his discretion, to anyone he liked. There were even complaints of favouritism.

To understand how this state of affairs had

come about, one has to consider the most unusual circumstances of those days. It was during the time of Partition that the Great Master passed away. The turmoil in which India found herself was almost without parallel. The exchange of population was one of the greatest mass migrations in the history of the world, added to which was extreme violence, widespread murder and the almost complete break-down of law and order.

In the midst of all this, the Great Master left his body, leaving a vacuum so great that the heart was taken out of the Dera and of all those remaining here. Many prominent satsangis and sevadars, being unable to withstand the pain and the heart-ache, even left the Dera and did not visit here again for many months.

Few could have felt this loss so keenly as Sardar Bahadur Ji himself. Though he was a model of moral rectitude, keen to impose discipline in every department of the Dera, his failing health was a great impediment in the implementation of his plans. Moreover, the long period of the Great Master's illness (October 1947 to April 2, 1948) had diluted the discipline and state of order at the Dera.

Sardar Bahadur Ji came out of his room only for satsang, and then sat in seva for half an hour in Lala Munshi Ram's office. For the rest of the day he was confined to his room. He was unable to give much attention to the day-to-day running of the administration due to his ill health.

Lala Munshi Ram was there, but he was virtually alone, and too meek and humble a person to assert his authority. He adopted a policy of least resistance, as in any case few listened to him. Apart from this, he was very busy settling the legal claims of the Dera, arising out of Partition, concerning satsang ghar properties left in Pakistan. Almost every day he had to attend one court or another. This kept him occupied most of the time.

Maharaj Ji, after coming to the Dera, pointed out this situation to Lala Munshi Ram. But he advised Maharaj Ji not to annoy the few haughty sevadars who were at the helm of affairs. "They will become a source of trouble for you," said Lala Munshi Ram, "and will create all sorts of obstacles in your way." So Maharaj Ji watched this unhappy situation helplessly, but not for long. After a year, he put his foot down.

The first step he took was to announce in satsang that nobody should take food outside the langar. Whoever wanted to eat must sit down and eat it in the langar. Naturally, to begin with, there was a considerable hue and cry, but he himself went to the langar every day at meal time to see that everything was served in an orderly fashion.

After another six months, Maharaj Ji announced in satsang that henceforth there would be no separate langar for Harijans.[1] All would eat together, and

---

1. "Harijan" is one of the names given to those considered by social prejudice to occupy the lowest echelon in the Indian caste system. Literally, "a man of God," a term originally coined by Mahatma Gandhi.

the Harijans would also cook and serve food along with everyone else. This was a radical step in those days of caste restriction and prejudice.

Therefore, to begin with, Maharaj Ji invited all the Dera sevadars and sadhus for a meal at his house. He sat down on the ground with all of them in a row and asked the Harijans to serve the food. Naturally, everyone was speechless. But they had no other alternative than to take part in the meal, and thus those who believed in caste restriction and feared public opinion, automatically had to rise above their prejudices. This was his way of handling a very ticklish problem.

At that time, Sardar Balwant Singh had recently retired from the Agricultural College in Lyallpur. Maharaj Ji called him and put him in charge of the afternoon seva and of the agricultural land. He also helped in the translation and publication of Sant Mat books into Punjabi. After some time, Mr. Bolakani also joined his team of loving sevadars and was put in charge of the construction and building works.

One of the first projects taken in hand was to construct a boundary wall around the Dera. There were deep ravines within and all around the colony, and besides there was no security to the colony, since it was open on all sides. Jackals, stray dogs and village cattle had full run of the Dera. The boundary wall was completed quite rapidly and the ravines were gradually filled over a period of time.

Amongst the buildings, Maharaj Ji once said, it was the Sadhu Ashram which was the first to be

BOUNDARY WALL AROUND DERA AND FILLING RAVINES

built. One day, Maharaj Ji visited the ravines in which many small caves had been excavated and where sadhus used to stay. It had rained heavily and a lot of rain water had entered the caves. Therefore the sadhus were living in great discomfort. Seeing their plight, Maharaj Ji was greatly moved and he thought of building some rooms for them, situated on the west of the Satsang Ghar.

When Maharaj Ji first approached Lala Munshi Ram and proposed this, he put up considerable resistance. Lala Munshi Ram had been serving the Dera for a very long time, since the days of the Great Master. He had seen the growth of the Dera practically from scratch, and naturally he had a great loyalty towards everything pertaining to it, including the finances. Because he had known Maharaj Ji since his childhood, he was perhaps over cautious in matters of spending during the first few years of Maharaj Ji's tenure. And because it was he who handled all the finances and accounts of the Dera, he pointed out to Maharaj Ji that there was not enough money in the Dera Bank accounts to take on the construction of buildings.

Maharaj Ji assured him that there was no cause for worry and that a lot of money would come in, suggesting that the progress of the building construction could proceed in stages, depending upon the finances available from the seva received.

Lala Munshi Ram had to agree, and the building work was started. No sooner had this happened, than money began pouring in, in seva, and the rooms were constructed very rapidly. Since it was originally meant for single sevadars and sadhus visiting or living in the Dera, it was called the Sadhu Ashram. Maharaj Ji said that after this, Lala Munshi Ram never again objected to any projects or proposals. And never since then has construction work stopped, even for a day, at the Dera.

As Maharaj Ji had mentioned, in 1951 there was hardly any Dera staff. Due to the lack of civic amenities, people had to go out to the river for toilet. They had to bathe there or with the water brought up from a well by a persian wheel. There was no electricity in the colony and no sewage system. Maharaj Ji's idea, therefore, was to build small houses with modern facilities to attract good sevadars, where people would be happy to live and feel comfortable. Mr. Bolakani, after his retirement, had already offered his services, and so with his help, the construction work was begun and the first colony of houses took shape.

Electricity was brought into the colony, a sewage system was built and all amenities were taken care of.

Masters have been—and still are—the real builders and administrators. Yet for obvious practical reasons, they need helpers as their instruments to run and make this colony what it is today. Those who live or visit here know it as Heaven on Earth. Gradually, as the colony developed, people began to offer their services after retirement. From amongst such people, Maharaj Ji chose Mr. Ahluwalia as his Secretary, to help the aging Lala Munshi Ram.

During that time, too, there was hardly any Sant

Mat literature available for the sangat. So thought was also given to publications.

In this way, gradually Maharaj Ji got everything into order and streamlined the administration. This naturally meant taking away the powers of the three sevadars who had once believed that they were running the Dera.

———

Sohan Singh Bhandari's reminiscences

Sohan Singh Bhandari was once reminiscing about the Great Master and how they all used to be with Maharaj Ji and Shoti, as children, playing and growing up together at the Dera. Later on, they worked together as members of the Sawan Service League, in the time of the Great Master.

He said that he was here when Maharaj Ji became the Master. It slipped out from his mouth that Maharaj Ji had been very reluctant to accept the office and had even run away from the Dera. But when we insisted that he should tell us more, he just kept quiet.

This remained in my mind and when the opportunity arose, I asked Maharaj Ji about it. Maharaj Ji reluctantly said, "It is true. I did try to run away, because I felt like a bird captured and kept in a cage. What bird wants to be caged? He always flutters and tries to get out of it. That is what I was trying to do."

———

A veiled hint about the successorship

One day Maharaj Ji recalled the sequence of events, in the autumn of 1951, which ultimately brought him to the Dera.

A few months before Sardar Bahadur Ji passed away, Maharaj Ji received a short note at his law office in Sirsa from Rai Sahib Munshi Ram, together with a form from the Imperial Bank of India (now the State Bank of India). The note asked him for his specimen signature on the form, in order to open a joint account at the Bank. Sardar Bahadur Ji's and Rai Sahib Munshi Ram's signatures were already there.

Maharaj Ji naturally wondered why his signatures were required. So he took the form to his father at Sikanderpur and showed it to him, asking if he knew the reason why his signatures were needed. Maharaj Ji's father advised him to do what was asked of him, and added that one should always obey the Masters, unquestioningly, since they know best.

It is well known that Maharaj Ji's father was a shining example of an obedient disciple. Even in the Great Master's time, although he was his son, he would carry out the Great Master's wishes implicitly without asking any questions.

Thus, as advised by his father, Maharaj Ji signed the bank papers and sent them back to Rai Sahib Munshi Ram, along with a letter saying that it would have been better if it had been made clear why the signatures were required.

Last days of Sardar Bahadur Ji—
Successorship

Sardar Bahadur Ji had been ailing for quite some time. For this reason, Maharaj Ji's father and mother had been at the Dera in October, 1951. But on the twenty-first of October, Sardar Bahadur Ji asked both of them to return to Sirsa, as he was feeling better. Obeying him, Maharaj Ji's parents left the Dera. His father left Beji (Maharaj Ji's mother) with relatives at Moga, and proceeded on to Sikanderpur. The same day, Maharaj Ji also arrived there, from Ambala.

After lunch, both of them were relaxing in the courtyard when a telegram was received saying, "Sardar Bahadur Ji serious, come immediately with Charan." Maharaj Ji's father was quite surprised, as he had left Beas only the previous day, and that too on the insistence of Sardar Bahadur Ji, who had assured him that he was better. Maharaj Ji also asked the same question of his father. His father also remarked to him, "Why are they calling you?" They started for Beas in Maharaj Ji's Hillman car, planning to pick up Beji from Moga.

But on the way from Sirsa to Moga, they found that the bridge at Otu was closed, due to a flood. They therefore had to make a detour of fifteen miles. While they were nearing Malout, the car broke down when the dynamo ceased functioning. It took two hours to repair, before they could resume their onward journey. Though by this time it was quite late in the night, they drove on.

Maharaj Ji told us that it must have been some time past midnight when he suddenly saw a flash of light and felt that Sardar Bahadur Ji was no more. Momentarily losing control of the car, it skidded, bringing it to a halt. Without saying anything else, he requested his father to drive, saying that he did not feel up to it.

So his father drove the car and they reached Moga in the early hours of the morning. Beji was quite surprised to see them, since she had left Beas only the day before, when Sardar Bahadur Ji had said that he was better. Anyway, within half an hour, after having had a wash, they left Moga for Beas.

On reaching Beas, they met Bibi Rali[1] and inquired about Sardar Bahadur Ji. She informed them that he had left his body soon after midnight. Bibi Rali further told both of them that Sardar Bahadur Ji had taken a promise from Rai Sahib Munshi Ram that the last rites would be performed without waiting for anyone and that his body should not be bathed, as he had already taken a bath. His last rites had been performed in the morning, according to his wishes, and everyone was at the cremation ground.

Maharaj Ji said that the thought of the successor did not even cross their minds at this juncture. So Maharaj Ji and his father started walking to the

---

1. Bibi Rali was in charge of the Great Master's kitchen. She was a child widow and was brought to the Dera by her father, a devoted disciple of Babaji.

cremation ground, about two miles away. They did not ask anyone about the successor, and they were not told anything about it by Bibi Rali.

As they were nearing the cremation ground, they saw Gian (Sardar Bahadur Ji's granddaughter) returning with Louise Hilger, and they noticed that Gian pointed out Maharaj Ji to Louise. When they reached the cremation ground, they found many satsangis present and from amongst them L.C. Dharmani, Randhir and Dharamdas came forward and bowed to Maharaj Ji. This naturally surprised him, for he did not understand why they should do this. Until this moment, Maharaj Ji said, the thought of a successor to Sardar Bahadur Ji had not occurred to him. At this point, however, an elderly satsangi from Balsarai—Jagat Singh— announced that the one who had been appointed by Sardar Bahadur Ji had come.

Suddenly, Maharaj Ji found the whole sangat paying their respects to him and following him until he reached the Great Master's house. By then, Maharaj Ji had realized that he was the one who had been appointed. His reactions during that day, written that very night in an old diary—in his own words and in his own hand—are heart-rending. They are given below, verbatim:

"On 22nd October on my return from Amballa, father received a telegram from Bibi Rali stating that Sardar Bahadur Maharaj ji's condition was serious & father should reach Beas at once along with myself. This news came to me as a great shock· but I consoled myself

thinking that at least I would have His Darshan. Father
& myself left by car at about midnight but just after
covering about 20 miles, something wrong went with
the car & we were detained for couple of hours there.

"While driving, suddenly my heart began sinking
& I felt that Beloved Master had left us. I could hardly
drive & so requested father 2 take my place.

"On reaching Dera at about 1-30 P.M. next day,
seeing so many Buses & Tongas people moving about in
disordered manner, my doubts were confirmed & this sad
news were delivered to me by Aman ji (Mrs. Kunda Singh)
We at once left for the River Bank where His last rites
were being performed. That place was about 4 miles from
Dera & it was a terrible trial for father to walk all
this distance. On the way, many people crossed me & some
showed unusual respect, which of course irritated me. On
reaching the spot, L. Dharam Chand from Amritsar *matha
tekya* [bowed with folded hands]. I understood what all
that meant. I was shocked & surprised to find
S. Bahadurji's order for me. People surrounded me & one
after another every body had his way. I hardly knew
what to do. I never felt so bad & so ashamed as I felt
then. I was feeling as if I had committed some henious
crime of my life & I had been punished with the sentence
of death & people have just surrounded me to see my
execution. It was terrible for me to spend three hours
there. Destiny could hardly play a worse jocke than
this. I knew I was not what I was taken to be & yet
I could not find any way out of this.

"Somehow I reached home & I know how terribly I wept confining myself to Maharaj ji's room. I fell out with Bhua Rali & protested with cries & tears in my eyes. On reaching home, I consoled my self in my mother's lap. I realised the worth of mother only then. Oh! No body should loose one's mother."

On 22nd October on my return
from Amballa, father Recieved
a telegram from Billu Rali
stating that Sardar Bahadur
Maharaj ji's Condition was serious
& father should reach Beas
at once along with my self.
This news came to me
as a great chock but I
Consoled my self thinking
that at least I would have
His Darshan. Father & my self
left by car at about (-
midnight but just after
Covering about 20 miles,
Something wrong went with
the car & we were detained
for couple of hours there.
       While driving suddenly
my heart began sinking
& I felt that Beloved master
had left us. I could

hardly drive & so requested father
to take my place.

On reaching Bera at
about 1-30. P. M. next day,
seeing so many Buses & Tongas
people moving about in disorder
manner, my doubts were
confirmed & these sad
news were g delivered to
me by Aman ji (Mrs. Kundalji)
We at once left for the
River Bank where his last
rites were being performed.
That place was about 4
miles from Bera & it was
a terrible terial for father to
walk all this distance. On
the way many people
crossed me & some showed
unusal respect which of
course irritated me. On
reaching the spot, L. Dharm

chand from Amritsar - ਵੀ ਚੰਦ.
I understood what all
that meant. I was shocked
& surprised to find S. Bahadur's
order for me. People
surrounded me & one after
another every body had his
way. I hardly knew what
to do. I never felt so bad
& so ashamed as I felt then.
I was feeling as if I had
committed some heinous
crime of my life & I had
been punished with the
sentence of death & people
have just surrounded me
to see my execution.
It was terrible for me
to spend three hours there.
Destiny could hardly
play a worst joke than
this. I knew I was not

what I was taken to be
& yet. I could not find
any way out of this.

Somehow I reached
home & I knew how
terribly I wept—confining
myself to Maharaj ji's room.
I fell out with Bhua Rah'
& protested with cries & tears
in my eyes. On reaching
home, I consoled myself
in my mother's lap. I realised
the worth of mother only then.
oh! no body should love
not mother.

He told us that he was surprised and shocked by Sardar Bahadur Ji's order. All his close relatives and friends surrounded him. Some of them were jubilant, others pitied him, and still others—particularly his relatives—sympathized with him. He wanted to be by himself and to be left alone, but in spite of his best efforts no one would leave him. Fed up with everybody and emotionally upset, he felt quite ashamed of creating such a scene.

In the evening, when everybody had gone to the Great Master's house to be with Bibi Rali, Maharaj Ji quietly called his nephew, Har Dayal, and asked him to park his car near Harbhaj's (shoe-maker's) shop. During those days this shop was outside the Dera. He borrowed money from his nephew, which turned out to be only twenty rupees, and quietly slipped out of his house, almost unnoticed in the darkness.

However, he was spotted by one of the sevadars (Kishan) who informed Sohan Singh Bhandari. Bhandari lost no time in joining Maharaj Ji who tried to put him off with one excuse or another, telling him that he was just taking a stroll.

But when Maharaj Ji reached the car, Bhandari became even more suspicious and watchful. Maharaj Ji again gave him an excuse, saying that he was going to the railway station to receive someone. So Bhandari insisted on accompanying him and slipped into the back seat of the car.

Maharaj Ji again requested him to leave him alone, as he wanted to be by himself, but Bhandari insisted on accompanying him. Maharaj Ji just did not know how to get rid of him. He said that he knew neither what he was doing, nor where he wanted to go. But he did immediately think of another plan for getting rid of Bhandari. He drove to Jullundur to Gurbux Singh Randhir's house, thinking that while Bhandari was talking to him, he would escape through the bathroom and quietly drive away. But somehow both of them understood the situation.

Much to Maharaj Ji's surprise and dismay, when he came out of the bathroom door he found Randhir lying in front of the car and Bhandari standing near the steering wheel. In spite of Maharaj Ji's pleading, they did not allow him to leave and said that if he wanted to drive away he must do so over their dead bodies. This drama continued for two hours. Ultimately, Maharaj Ji drove back to the Dera, reaching there around 2 a.m.

In the meantime, there was considerable hue and cry in the Dera when he was found to be missing. Everyone was searching for him—on the river bank, in the deep ravines, in every nook and corner of the Dera. All the members of the family were awake, upset and weeping.

Everyone must have heaved a sigh of relief when he again made his appearance at 2 a.m. His parents decided to take him to Sirsa to give him time to compose himself, and they informed Lala Munshi Ram accordingly.

Excerpts from letters

The next day he was driven to Sirsa, with Lala Munshi Ram. Maharaj Ji says that what happened at Sirsa is very difficult to narrate. Some idea of his feelings during that time can be gleaned from letters which he wrote in his own hand to his friends.

October 24th, 1951, Beas

"On reaching here at 2 p.m. yesterday, we find that once again we have become orphans. Beloved Maharaj Ji left us early yesterday morning and we could only watch his last ceremony being performed by the satsangis.

"I am almost dead too. I have been declared dead minus existence. Destiny has played the biggest joke with me.

". . . as I am feeling now, facing people with folded hands, eyes full with tears and sorrow. When I compare my shortcomings with their faith, devotion and respect—my mind ceases to think and I am living as if I have no other alternative. . . I have been surrounded, captured and imprisoned.

". . . All my patience and tolerance seem to have been exhausted. I am at war within myself and can hardly decide anything . . . yet destiny had made me face all that. I wish I could be cruel and quite ignorant of others' wishes. Then I would not have been cruel to myself. . . . Just spending the days as they come before me."

October 26th, 1951

"I have not been able to make up my mind till yet—perhaps I may be able to decide under Sirsa atmosphere. . . . I hardly know what to do. . . .You need not worry much. Whatever there will be in my destiny, I will reap it.

October 30th, 1951, Sirsa

"SIRSA
30.10.51

"My dear.

"I am feeling quite normal now The news took me as the greatest surprise of my life & nature perhaps could not give me worse shock than this

"As for not accepting this, there is nothing in my hand now to accept or reject it My rejection will not make any difference for the Satsangies & I would be haunted anywhere I go. I cannot go underground even— as after I came back the position will be the same. All my kith & kin, friends & relatives are advising me to take this responsibility & I should be prepared to make any sacrifice that this office demands My wife & all others have assured me of their full co-operation & now I find no other way but to carry out Hazur Maharaj ji's wishes & pray to Him to make me worthy of that.

"Yours affl
Charan"

SIKSA

30.10.51

My dear.

I am feeling quite normal now. The news took me as the greatest surprise of my life & nature perhaps could not give my more shock than this

As for not accepting
this, there is nothing in
my hand now to accept
or reject & my rejection
will not make any difference
in the Sat Sangees & I would
be haunted anywhere I
go. I cannot go under-
ground even — as after
I come back the
position will be the
same. All my kith &
kin, friends & relations
are advising me to take
this responsibility & I
should be prepared to

make any sacrifice that this
office demands. My wife & all
others have assured me of
their full co-operation & now
I find no other way but to
carry out Heaven Maharaj's D.S
wishes & pray to Him to make
me worthy of that.

"Yours aff^t^
Charan"

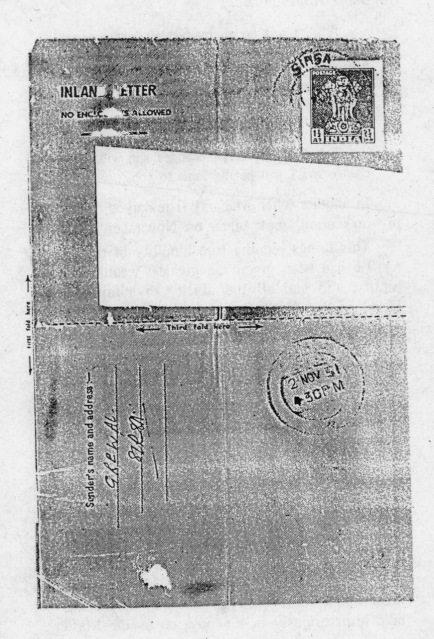

November 7th, 1951, Beas

". . . I had no alternative left but to accept this heavy responsibility. You can well imagine how hard it will be to carry it out. This has created many other complications and I hardly find any clue to them. I have entirely submitted to Him—His will—and will face whatever He has in store for me. But I want to assure you all, and particularly yourself, that I have not changed and will never change and I will be the same to you. . . ."

In another letter Maharaj Ji remarked, "Anyhow, my 'execution' took place on November 4th."

This brings out the true humility of his character. He had been given the greatest wealth of spirituality, and had all the ability to administer the Dera, as the Master—which he truly deserved to become. Still, he neither wanted nor desired the position. All this happened as stipulated in the registered will of Sardar Bahadur Ji, who acted according to the inner dictates of his own Master, as well as those of the preceding Masters.

———

Early days as Master

In the beginning, Maharaj Ji found it hard to bring the old satsangis round to helping him with the Dera administration. All of them had seen him as a child with the Great Master. They had seen him grow into a young lawyer. As such they could not take him seriously in his position as the Master.

In this connection, I heard an interesting story from Professor Jagmohan Lal. The Professor, an old satsangi from the time of the Great Master, was also one of the present Master's professors from his college days. He was staying at the Dera when Maharaj Ji came to the 'gaddi'.[1] Professor Sahib used to tell me never to forget that he is a perfect Master, and to emphasize this point he narrated to me his own experience.

In those earlier days, Maharaj Ji called him to his house to dictate a few letters to some foreigners, replies to whom were long overdue. But somehow, the Professor did not take Maharaj Ji's request seriously. After all, he had been one of his students whom he had watched growing up. So instead of going to Maharaj Ji, he sat in meditation; and this happened consecutively for three days. Every day, Maharaj Ji would ask him to come to his house, and instead he would attend to meditation.

On the fourth day, the same pattern was repeated. The Professor sat in bhajan, but the Shabd— instead of pulling him up, started pushing him out. In spite of his best efforts, he could not succeed. Then it dawned on him that this was happening to him because of his disobedience to the Satguru. So he got up, went to Maharaj Ji, and asked for his forgiveness. Thereafter, he did whatever was desired of him.

A similar incident was narrated to me by

---

1. Literally,'gaddi' means a cushion. In this context, 'coming to the gaddi' means the installation of a Master.

Mr. Ahluwalia who became Maharaj Ji's first secretary. He had been the manager of the Imperial Bank of India (now the State Bank of India), but had retired. Meanwhile, his elder son had joined the bank and was posted to Ambala City as manager. Mr. Ahluwalia was living with him, and whenever Maharaj Ji passed Ambala City, he would visit him at his son's house.

One day, Maharaj Ji requested him to come to the Dera and help Rai Sahib Munshi Ram, who was getting old. Mr. Ahluwalia promised Maharaj Ji that he would do so. However, upon retirement, he thought that first he would go to Calcutta to help his other son to get a job, as he had many influential friends there.

He stayed in Calcutta for a month. But everyone whom he approached, disappointed him. Ultimately, he was so disillusioned that he left his son in Calcutta to find a job by himself, and took a train to the Dera with the intention of serving Maharaj Ji. Actually, he had had a dream in which the Great Master had appeared to him and said, "Why are you delaying going to Charan? (Maharaj Ji). He has requested you to come, many times. Do you think you can get a job for your son?" Mr. Ahluwalia told me that he felt greatly ashamed, and while he was on the train to Beas, at some midstation, he got a telegram from his son saying that he had got a job.

This is frequently found to be the case, that when we attend to the Master's work our worldly needs are automatically taken care of. However, if we run after the world, we may lose the worldly as well as the spiritual wealth. Maharaj Ji sometimes quotes the Great Master, who used to say, "If you want chairs, bring a carpenter home to stay with you." Similarly, whatever we may need in this world will be forthcoming if we bring the Lord 'home'—if we realize him within ourselves. Then all his gifts will automatically come to us.

The early days at the Dera were quite hard for Maharaj Ji, for he had to streamline the entire administration. Today, one sees a well-planned, beautiful, clean township with greenery and trees all around. One almost feels as though one is in a beautiful resort. However, what the Dera was like when Maharaj Ji took over is difficult to describe, unless one had seen it in those days, during the early fifties.

Under his able guidance and masterly planning, it has grown steadily. Those who saw the ravines in those days, wonder where they have disappeared. Today, the major part of the colony stands upon those filled-in ravines. The river too, which once had the International Guest House on its banks, has changed its course and moved farther away leaving behind hundreds of acres of fertile land—'the Mund'. This was all achieved by the loving seva of the sangat, performed for their beloved Master under his divine guidance. It is a rare example of love and devotion.

There is no one like him on the face of this earth. One realizes this when one comes to his feet. Humility, generosity, kindness, love personified—

one falls short of words to describe him. How
he takes care of everyone, rich and poor alike,
with such thoughtfulness and consideration is
unbelievable.

His remarkable memory

He has one characteristic in particular which
never ceases to amaze us. He never forgets
anyone—it does not matter how many years
have passed since he last saw someone—whether
the person was his acquaintance from college or
school days, or from his childhood. Also, whenever anyone approaches him for help of any kind,
it is readily forthcoming, irrespective of whether
the person is a satsangi or not—that never matters
to him.

He meets people on the basis of the relationship which existed at the time he came to know
them. To give an example, it happened recently that
one of his close friends from his college days, a
non-satsangi, met him after a period of thirty years.
Yet Maharaj Ji greeted him with the same warmth
and showered on him the same love and affection
which he had had for him in their college days.
Though he was now the Master, Maharaj Ji treated
him and behaved with him just like a friend—there
was no difference at all. In fact, this friend later
lived with him, as a member of the family, for his
wife died and there was no one to take care of him.

This is his divinity personified. What greater proof does one need in these days, when people do not care for their own kith and kin, not to mention their friends?

_____

A perfect disciple

In one of the foreigners' meetings, someone asked Maharaj Ji if the Great Master was his grandfather. He replied, "Yes," and added with great emphasis, "but he was also my Master, and that is more important." This speaks volumes concerning his relationship with the Great Master. Whenever he speaks of the Great Master his eyes well up with tears and his voice becomes choked. This happens in conversation, and more so when he refers to the Great Master in satsang. Such is his deep love for his beloved Master.

_____

Great Master's wisdom

Today, Maharaj Ji was telling us about some of the qualities of the Great Master. He described the Great Master as a man of exceptional wisdom and thoughtfulness in all his dealings with people. Maharaj Ji illustrated this with the following incident, which happened when he was a young man.

Maharaj Ji had got himself a new tonga, and one weekend he travelled in it from Sirsa to Sikanderpur, on a visit. In those days, this was the only

conveyance which could go from the main road to
the house and farm, since the road was neither
paved nor tarred.[1] Maharaj Ji's father owned an old
'buck-board', which is like a carriage.

When at Sikanderpur, it was Great Master's
routine to go to the farm and the sugar mill every
morning. Maharaj Ji strongly wished the Great
Master to go in his tonga and managed to have his
request conveyed to him through Shadi, the Great
Master's personal attendant.

While the Great Master was getting ready to go,
Maharaj Ji's father was standing near his 'buck-
board', in which to take the Great Master to the
farm. So when Shadi conveyed Maharaj Ji's request,
the Great Master looked at him and his new tonga,
but went towards the 'buck-board', saying: "One's
own son is the best of sons, one's own husband is
the best of men amongst men."

(ਆਪਣਾ ਪੂਤ ਸਪੂਤ ਹੈ ਆਪਣਾ ਕੰਤ ਸੁਕੰਤ)

Maharaj Ji's father drove the Great Master away
to the farm and the sugar mill. Naturally, Maharaj Ji
was greatly disappointed and his face fell, but he
did not say anything. The next weekend, he again
came to Sikanderpur in his tonga. As usual, in the
morning the Great Master got ready to go to the
farm and the sugar mill. Maharaj Ji stood near his
tonga and his father had the 'buck-board' ready.

---

1. In fact, in those days there was really no road between the
main road and the village; it was a huge space of brambles and dust
so thick that there were no tracks left from any vehicle, for one to
follow.

MAHARAJ JI AS A BRIDEGROOM WITH HIS BROTHER

Maharaj Ji did not have the courage to get his request repeated.

The Great Master—to the great joy of Maharaj Ji—got into his tonga, saying to Shadi, "Interest is dearer than the principal."

(ਮੂਲ ਨਾਲੋਂ ਬਿਆਜ ਪਿਆਰਾ)

"Such was His astuteness," said Maharaj Ji.

There is another incident which is quite interesting, showing the Great Master's deep insight into human nature and his way of dealing with difficult situations, people, and problems.

A proposal was made for the marriage of Rao Sahib's daughter to Maharaj Ji. Now, the Great Master knew that his eldest son, Sardar Bachint Singh (Maharaj Ji's uncle) would object to this match because Rao Sahib was a Hindu, as well as being from Uttar Pradesh (U.P.). In those days, in the Punjab it was considered below one's dignity to marry outside one's community or province.

So, the Great Master very tactfully approached his elder son, and told him that a proposal had come from Rao Sahib for the marriage of his daughter, and asked if—in his opinion—the proposal could be accepted on behalf of Gur Dayal (Sardar Bachint Singh's grandson).

Rao Sahib was well known amongst the satsangis, and therefore Sardar Bachint Singh immediately agreed, saying that there would be no harm in accepting the proposal, as Rao Sahib was an influential and rich 'zamindar' (landlord).

The Great Master replied that the horoscopes of the boy and girl would have to be matched, as the people from U.P. believed in these things and never arranged marriages of their daughters unless the partners were well matched. He said that he would have this done at Beas.

On his return to Beas, he called Sardar Bhagat Singh, who was very close to the Great Master. Usually, the Great Master would seek his advice, on family matters as well as on Dera affairs. Sardar Bhagat Singh also knew how to draw up horoscopes. So the Great Master, taking him into confidence, asked him to send a telegram to Sardar Bachint Singh, saying that the horoscopes did not match. The matter was therefore dropped.

When Sardar Bachint Singh next visited the Dera, the Great Master suggested to him that since his grandson's horoscope did not tally, what would he say if they were to try Charan's (Maharaj Ji's), since he (Sardar Bachint Singh) did consider their family to be a good one. Naturally, the Great Master's son had no option but to reply in the affirmative.

This demonstrates the Great Master's deep understanding of human nature. He accomplished whatever he wanted without offending or hurting anyone's feelings. In this case, even if he had ordered it, no one would have disobeyed him. Yet he got the acceptance first, and then proceeded.

There are several incidents which also show that Maharaj Ji follows the same methods, some of

which are narrated amongst these pages, such
as the integration of Harijans in the langar, and
his handling of Lala Munshi Ram. Maharaj Ji
possesses the same wisdom, never hurting or offending anybody, though he has to deal with a large
number of Dera staff members, government officials,
politicians, journalists, etc.

With the manifold increase in the sangat and the
multifarious activities going on at the Dera, the
problems which come before Maharaj Ji are many
and at times, complex. However, with his deep
insight into human nature, and his perfect human
relations, Maharaj Ji is able to deal with all problems and people with a rare sense of wisdom. He
never hurts anyone, yet the work gets done, though
all this means a great strain on him.

Today it can be said with pride that the Dera
is a unique institution, enjoying singular prestige
and a high reputation not only with the government,
but also with various other bodies. This is all due
to Maharaj Ji's foresight, wisdom and humane
approach.

Manifold increase in sangat

Someone once pointed out to Maharaj Ji that
satsangis have increased more than ten-fold since he
came to the 'gaddi'. He replied, "This is the result
of the seed sown by Soami Ji and his successors.

We are not even able to water and nourish all that they have sown." Maharaj Ji always gives the example of the banyan tree. Its seed may be very small, he says, yet it grows into a huge tree. Looking at the size of the tree, one wonders at the small size of the seed. Therefore, whatever one sees today, Maharaj Ji says, is all a result of the Great Master and his predecessors' sowing of the seed. All this is the result of his humility, love for and dedication to his own Master.

Give rather than receive

Another incident which Maharaj Ji narrated was of the time just before the Great Master passed away. The Great Master called his sons and their families and said, "I have settled you all independently and well. Now you are all earning, I would like to advise all of you, 'Never spread your hand to receive, always extend it to give.' " His sons replied, "By your blessings, it will be as you desire."

Today, every satsangi knows how much Maharaj Ji and his family give in seva from their farm. This is a continuing process. They have given land for the satsang ghar at Sikanderpur, and have also given land to the Radha Soami Satsang Beas Society for constructing a charitable hospital.

NEVER SPREAD YOUR HAND TO RECEIVE

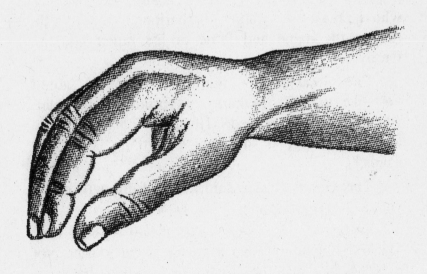

ALWAYS EXTEND IT TO GIVE

Three types of sons

Maharaj Ji once narrated in satsang an incident concerning the Great Master which was quite an eye-opener for us. One day, the Great Master called Maharaj Ji and his brother (Shoti), and put a question to both of them, asking, "What would you like to become—a son, a bad son, or a good son?"

Maharaj Ji replied that he did not fully understand the question.

The Great Master explained that a 'son' (ਪੁੱਤਰ) is the son who inherits from his father all the land, wealth, reputation and goodwill of the family, and keeps it intact, neither increasing it nor squandering it. A 'bad son' (ਕਪੁਤਰ) is the son who squanders the inheritance he had received from his father and loses it, while a 'good son' (ਸਪੁਤਰ) is the son who increases his father's inheritance and wealth, raising the name and fame of his father and the family.

The Great Master again asked, "What would you like to be?" Maharaj Ji's brother kept quiet, while Maharaj Ji replied, "Huzur, of course I would like to be a 'good son', but everything is in your hands."

The Great Master said, "The Lord will make you a 'very good son'." (ਸਪੁਤਰ)

Today we can see what a 'very good son' Maharaj Ji has been and is to the Great Master. Not only has the material wealth increased a thousand-fold, but the increase in the dissemination of the

MAHARAJ JI AND HIS MOTHER

spiritual wealth seems to have no limit. The Great Master's teachings have reached every nook and corner of the world through the selfless service and dedication of Maharaj Ji.

Maharaj Ji's relationship with his mother

Maharaj Ji's relationship with his mother, whom he lovingly calls 'Beji,' is unique. This is another great trait of his character. The love and respect he gives to her is touching and at the same time exemplary. In these days of materialism and selfishness, relationships have lost their value, and no one really cares for anyone, anymore. But the care Maharaj Ji takes of his mother, and the consideration he shows to her, with genuine love, is to be seen to be believed. In fact, the first thing in the morning, before starting his daily schedule, he goes to her, and touches her feet. He greets her and spends a little time with her.

In this connection, how true the words of Maharaj Ji's father have become. During his last days, Maharaj Ji's father told Beji that he had not given her any property or cash. He added, "Even if I had given it to you, it would not have lasted you for very long. But I have given real 'wealth' to you—your two loving and devoted sons. I assure you that they will not only look after you, but will even attend to all your responsibilities and needs in life, without your even having to ask." After saying this, he took hold of one of Beji's hands and placed it in the hands of Maharaj Ji (the elder son), telling her, "You will never feel a want of anything."

All this has come true. Maharaj Ji and his brother arranged the marriage of their younger sister. The other three sisters were married earlier. They also educated their widowed elder sister's children, arranged their marriages, and got them settled in life. Beji has always had full control of the household at Sikanderpur. Her every wish has been a command for her sons, who never questioned but only obeyed her. Which mother is so fortunate as to have such sons, in present times?

For the last two years, Beji has not been keeping too well. Although she is a lady of strong will power and strong constitution, yet at this age, in her nineties, it is difficult for her to take frequent journeys. Maharaj Ji brought her to the Dera from Sikanderpur, so that she can be looked after, under his supervision. In spite of his busy daily schedule these days, he still finds enough time to spend with her. Every day he takes his meals with her, makes her laugh, and tries to keep her cheerful and comfortable. It is amazing that in present times there are such devoted sons.

Maharaj Ji is perfection personified, truly a divine being, flawless in every respect. Words cannot describe him. From whatever angle one sees him—as a brother, father, husband, son, friend and of course as a Master—he is matchless, and a true friend of humanity.

Love and darshan

The following are extracts from Maharaj Ji's advice, given to an American satsangi lady, concerning the benefits of the darshan of the Master's physical form. This was sometime in 1952 and I came across it just today.

Saints attach great importance to having the darshan of a living Master. To derive bliss from the mere darshan of the Master is a great thing, as it indicates that the disciple has love, and that he desires nothing except to have more and more darshan. He is always anxious to have as much darshan of the Master as possible, which ultimately results in drawing the disciple closer to the Master on the inner plane.

Maharaj Ji added that sometimes the Master imparts the wealth of spirituality to some particular disciple without any apparent effort on the part of the disciple. But the right to this grace may have been earned in past lives.

More important than meditation are love and devotion. Love is complete in itself. In love, the lover becomes one with the beloved. There is no meditation greater than love. There is no law higher than love, and there is no goal beyond love. God and love are the same thing. Meditation involves effort; in love, all is spontaneous. Love means merging into the Shabd—losing one's identity.

Love differs from lust. Lust pulls us down, while love lifts us up. In lust, there is suffering, in love there is union and joy. Lust is the craving of the senses, love is the ardour of the soul. Lust is an instrument of Kal; love is the gift of the Master. Love, awakened by the Master, is a rare privilege, and leads to salvation.

This reminds me that Maharaj Ji once told us in one of the English meetings that before coming to the 'gaddi', he had never read a Sant Mat book, although from his childhood he had been brought up at the Dera by Bibi Rali, under the loving guidance of the Great Master. But with the love which he felt for the Great Master and for Sardar Bahadur Ji, he never felt the need to read any book. He said, "I know Sant Mat through the Great Master—whatever he said was Sant Mat for me. But you people know the Master through the books, through the teachings."

Once he told Sardar Bahadur Ji, "Your satsangs are very short," because Sardar Bahadur Ji used to hold satsang for only forty-five minutes. At this, Sardar Bahadur Ji replied, "I have been a professor all through my life, and I know that no one can concentrate for more than forty-five minutes."

On hearing this, Maharaj Ji told him, "But who goes there to hear the satsang? We go there to have your darshan!" At this, Sardar Bahadur Ji just smiled, for he knew that the words came from the heart of a perfect disciple who was to become the Master.

Once, during one of the English meetings, someone asked Maharaj Ji about darshan. Maharaj Ji replied, "It is the helplessness of a disciple to look at his beloved. One should never calculate that darshan will result in spiritual gain. True darshan is to lose one's identity and merge oneself in the Master with no expectation, desire or wish. Just to go on looking at the Master helplessly—that is darshan."

Extracts of letters on Maharaj Ji between his friends

I recently came across some interesting comments concerning Maharaj Ji, in correspondence between two of his friends.

"It is a tragedy that whereas my love for him grows, he is quite contented to keep his golden silence. At least, so it appears. Not that he can ever give up his love for me or anyone else whom he has ever loved once in life. That is his weakness, and therein also lies his greatness. You know and I just understand."

At the end, a postscript is added to this letter:

"I am glad to add, this letter had a quick result—there is a letter from him today."

In another letter, this same friend wrote, while travelling with Maharaj Ji:

"I am poor and yet I have to pay to be with him. I am in the background struggling to be nearer, I am happy all the same. He (Maharaj Ji) has his ways to compensate and there he is generous. You are the same in another way. At least we all understand. This God-man is a strange being. He is simple and yet most complicated. But he is ours,

isn't it? So we are happy. He is great. People
respect him, love him and are won by his person-
ality and charm."

Extracts from Maharaj Ji's letters

In an extract from one of Maharaj Ji's letters to
a friend, he writes:

"I do not know, but whenever I leave India, a
strange philosopher's mood overtakes me, and I
hardly feel that anything belongs to me there.
Whenever I leave those 'blessed surroundings', I
feel that I have never belonged to them at all. I
always have to force myself to believe that I have
some responsibilities and liabilities, and so-called
attachments there. So now you can understand the
cause of my silence. The more I see the world and
its people, the more I feel I do not belong to it. I
always long to remain within myself, I feel my
world is my own—quite different from what I see
around me."

The following is another excerpt from one of
Maharaj Ji's letters, dated January 23rd, 1963:

"Physically and mentally I am dead, though
living. Maharaj Ji's mission has reached every
corner of the world, but I have done a mess with
myself and my health. I do not want to fail in my
duty nor do I want to be short in the expectations
of my Beloved Master. I have given to the people
all I have. What I could not give, I just did not
have. All that I am doing is just with a sense of
duty and out of love for my Beloved. If anyone
cares to follow my daily routine—minute by

minute—then only one can know what I am going through. Right from 8th September till today, I have not slept continuously for one week under one roof and this is to continue till the end of May. I am very much pressed to visit U.S.A. in this summer."

***

In spite of Maharaj Ji's busy schedule, he is always considerate to his friends and tries to find time to write to them. His thoughtfulness and concern are unbelievable. To one of his friends, he wrote:

"I appreciate your love very much, and I know what it means for you to be away from me for such a long time. Probably for the first time in your life you have had to experience all this. But then you must have a practical view on life. You have certain commitments in your life, and it makes me happy that you are able to meet them smilingly. I am sorry I cannot keep up with your rapid correspondence, but my thoughts are mostly with you.

"The Dera is expanding with very fast speed. I have to cope with its day to day activities."

In a letter to one of his friends, dated October 22nd, 1964, Maharaj Ji wrote:

"Please do not feel that I am ignoring both of you, and that you do not command my love and friendship any more. Whoever has made way to my heart will ever stay there."

In another letter to a friend dated April 22nd, 1962, he wrote from abroad:

"I am taking Huzur Maharaj Ji's mission to
these countries, and his hand of grace will always
be with me. Please have no worry on this score. He
is always merciful on this sinner."

It was Maharaj Ji's unassuming humility that
though he was doing everything, he would invariably
attribute it to his Master.

———

Sardar Bahadur Ji — reflections

Regarding friends, Maharaj Ji told us another
incident about Sardar Bahadur Ji. Once, at the Dera,
Maharaj Ji was going with some friends towards the
office where Sardar Bahadur Ji was sitting. While
walking, they were teasing a friend to the extent that
he was almost in tears. Sardar Bahadur Ji was
watching all this, and beckoned Maharaj Ji with his
finger. He said gently, "Chowdhry," as he fondly
called Maharaj Ji, "one should joke in such a manner that the other person enjoys it as much as you
enjoy it."

(ਮਖੌਲ ਉਹ ਹੁੰਦਾ ਹੈ ਜਿਸਦਾ ਜਿੰਨਾ ਕਰਨ ਵਾਲਾ ਸੁਆਦ ਲੈਂਦਾ ਹੈ, ਉਨਾਂ ਹੀ ਜਿਸ ਨਾਲ
ਕੀਤਾ ਜਾਵੇ, ਉਹ ਸੁਆਦ ਲਵੇ)

Sardar Bahadur Ji was very simple and a man
of few words. He always spoke briefly and to the
point. During the Great Master's time, he would
always sit quietly in a corner and just gaze at the
beloved face of the Great Master, while discussions
would go on with the staff members concerning the

land and other Dera matters. Everybody would take part in the discussions, and suddenly the Great Master would look at Sardar Bahadur Ji and ask, "What is your opinion?" and the reply would always be, "Who knows better than you, Huzur?" And the Great Master would just smile.

Maharaj Ji told us that a little while after coming to the 'gaddi', Sardar Bahadur Ji went to Sirsa, for a visit. Maharaj Ji was there, and so were all his sisters, as well as Beji. Every morning, the family used to go to him to pay their respects. Sardar Bahadur Ji did not know the names of Maharaj Ji's sisters and how many of them there were, in spite of the fact that he was very close to Maharaj Ji's parents. So he asked Maharaj Ji how many sisters he had. Maharaj Ji replied, "Four." "How many are married?" was the next question, and the reply was, "Two." Then he asked Maharaj Ji their names, as he wished to express intimacy by addressing them personally.

But when they all came in the morning, as usual, to pay their respects, Satnam became Gurnam, and Gurnam became Devi and Devi became Mahinder. So Maharaj Ji just smiled and pointed out their correct names to him. But by the next day he could call them all by their correct names.

***

On one occasion, talking about Sardar Bahadur Ji, Maharaj Ji said, "Once I had come to the Dera

and was sitting with him, when he asked me about
one of my friends. I told him that I did not see him
anymore, and that there was no friendship now.

"On hearing this, Sardar Bahadur Ji told me,
'Once a friend is always a friend. If you go on
testing your friends, you will be friendless.'"

———

Development of the langar

Recently in the morning satsang, Maharaj Ji told
us some of the history of the langar. He said that
during his lifetime, Babaji had asked the Great
Master to hold satsang and to take care of the Dera
administration after he had departed. So when the
Great Master succeeded Babaji, he said: "My first
and foremost problem was that Babaji had started
the free langar during his lifetime—so how to keep
it running? Considerable funds for foodgrains were
required to keep it going, and I personally had
never made any appeal for any donation of any
kind, not even when I was president or a member
of various religious, social and charitable organizations during my service days.

"So I prayed to Babaji inside, 'Huzur, you have
started the langar. I have always lived within the
limit of my income and have never asked anyone
for anything. How can I run such a huge langar?'
and he assured me, 'You need not worry on this
account. This has been started with the blessings of

LANGAR

LANGAR

Soami Ji Maharaj—you keep it running as it is and there will never be any food shortage, at any time. It will always be in abundance.' "

With Babaji's grace and blessings, the langar has always run during the Great Master's time, during Sardar Bahadur Ji's time and, as everyone knows how today, when the sangat has increased by hundreds of thousands, the langar is open and food is served all the time.

Maharaj Ji continued, "I have seen the langar operating even during times of war and at the terrible time of partition with Pakistan, when there was a shortage of foodgrains, everywhere. A large number of refugees coming from Pakistan, as well as those going from India on their way to Pakistan, had all gathered at the Dera. Yet the langar continued just as it does now.

"During the time of partition, the Great Master had ordered that cooked food should also be supplied to all the refugees at the Beas railway station, whether they were coming from Pakistan or were on their way to Pakistan (irrespective of whether they were Muslims or Hindus). So every train-load was well fed, and the satsangis were happy to serve them.

"I do not know how and from where all this food came. Right from my childhood I have always seen the langar storehouse full of grain. Now, there is ample grain in our stocks and a great deal more than our needs, in spite of the fact that lakhs and lakhs of people are fed in the free langar every day, especially during our monthly satsangs. It is all

thanks to the love and devotion of the sangat. The
Dera management does not have to buy any foodgrains from the market.

"The Great Master often used to say that Babaji
has laid the foundation of this Dera on love and
seva."

This is evident these days, from what we see
here, all around us. Lakhs[1] of people have their
meals in the langar during the bhandara time.
Sevadars cook and serve the food with great love
and devotion. It is a sight which has to be seen to
be believed. When Maharaj Ji goes for his round to
the langar during the bhandara time, the sevadarnis
(lady sevadars) cook, sing shabds, and with folded
hands, tears rolling from their eyes, have Maharaj
Ji's darshan. It is a moving and beautiful experience.
Love and devotion are transparent on the faces of
the sevadars. They are so happy with the few moments of darshan which they have! One can see the
contentment on their faces which comes only from
seva.

The langar at the bhandara time is truly unique,
for I do not think that anywhere else in the world
is free food served to such multitudes. 50,000 people
sit down at a time and are served food. This number is repeated several times over, at each meal, for
at the bhandaras, several hundred thousand people
gather here. The cleanliness after each meal, where
people eat, is unbelievable.

It is also well known that the size of the

---

1. One lakh equals one hundred thousand.

sangat at bhandara times is increasing from year to year. On certain peak days during those times, there may be four or five hundred thousand people visiting the Dera, perhaps even more. The highest estimates have most of the time been exceeded. It is obvious that the number of people eating in the langar also goes up accordingly, and is more than expected. The langar storehouses, however, have never been exhausted, and a shortage of food has never been felt, on any single day. Such is the grace of the Masters.

Planning for Maharaj Sawan Singh Charitable Hospital, Beas

When the plans were being drawn up for construction of the Maharaj Sawan Singh Charitable Hospital at Beas, its estimated cost was placed at around three crores of rupees (30 millions). The Dera did not have adequate funds at that time, so naturally, all the Dera officials got worried and asked Maharaj Ji how the Dera could afford to take up such a big project. Maharaj Ji replied, "The Great Master will look after it; wait and see." Not only did the hospital get completed and fully equipped, but also the funds available to the Maharaj Jagat Singh Medical Relief Society, which runs the hospital, have exceeded far beyond the imagination of anyone.

A satsangi narrated the following incident to

me, concerning the hospital. During the construction
of the hospital, a need arose for certain types of
steel which were in short supply in the market,
thereby hampering progress. The necessary steel
components were available from the Tata Iron
and Steel Co., so Maharaj Ji asked this satsangi,
who had contacts amongst some of the top directors
at Tatas, to meet them and get the requisite amount
of steel. The satsangi went to Mr. Naval Tata and
explained to him about the hospital project. Mr. Tata
thought that his company was being approached
for a donation, and asked the satsangi what amount
he expected. When the satsangi explained that he
had not come to ask for any donation, but only
for an allotment of steel on a priority basis, moreover payment would be made in cash, Mr. Tata was
wonderstruck. He said, "You say that a hospital
costing three crore rupees is being constructed,
yet you do not want any donation? It is unbelievable. I am presently constructing a hospital
costing only seventy lakh rupees. I am collecting
donations for that, and I am finding it difficult."

Of course, Tatas made the steel available
for our hospital. But the point is that with Maharaj
Ji's grace, money has never been a problem for
any project he has taken up, however big it might
have been. This happens even in spite of the fact
that no one at the Dera ever asks for a donation from anyone. All the money comes in volun-
tarily.

Often, Maharaj Ji has turned down big contribu-
tions from millionaires in India and abroad. During

one of Maharaj Ji's trips abroad, a non-satsangi billionaire—a non-resident Indian—once offered Maharaj Ji a blank cheque, requesting him to fill in any amount he liked and to accept it as a donation for the hospital. Maharaj Ji politely declined to accept the cheque.

———

Diary entries — father's death

Today I came across one of Maharaj Ji's old diaries written in his own hand, from which the following excerpts are given below, concerning the departure of his father from this world.

July 7th, 1956

Father made his will giving Sikanderpur land to Cuckoo and Rana, and Darbi Rasulpur to Harjit. Gives Rs. 1000/- to Sarwan (an old servant) for services rendered to him.

Entrusts Mother's hand to me.

May Maharaj Ji make me worthy of this trust.

He is very anxious to leave his body.

July 9th

Father's condition quite serious.

July 11th

Things are happening which are not pleasant to face. Bhua Rakhi died at 2.30 a.m.

July 17th

Sadhu Singh, who filed a civil suit against me a few years ago, has apologized. I never had any grouse against him.

August 5th

Father is very peaceful. He says that Maharaj Ji is always with him, and is very happy.

August 8th

Father asked me to look after the family, after him.

August 14th

Father called me and asked, "How many days are there in Sankrant?" He seems to be ready to leave on that day.

August 15th

Father asks for passport. He says he is ready to leave.

(When asked regarding the passport, Maharaj Ji replied, "My father said to me smilingly that the Great Master says (inside), 'You should ask Charan for the passport and after that I will give you the visa.' ")

August 16th

I left for Moga at 11 a.m. after the Sankrant satsang, and came back at 6 p.m. Father died in my absence at 12.45 noon.

August 17th

Father cremated in the morning. I held satsang after the cremation.

On reading this, my curiosity was aroused and so I asked Maharaj Ji, when he knew that his father was going to leave the body, why did he leave and go to Moga. Maharaj Ji answered, "My mother was very much attached to my father. But my father was absolutely detached and his attention was inside. So I thought that if Beji remained with him at the time of his death, she might draw his attention out by talking about some trivial family matters.

"Then, in the morning newspaper, I read that her brother had died at Moga, giving me a genuine excuse to take her away. So I suggested, 'Let us visit the family to offer our condolences—it will only take a few hours.' Beji agreed, but I had to take her, as she would have refused to go with anyone else."

Naming the children

This brought to mind an interesting incident concerning Maharaj Ji, related to me by Professor Jagmohan Lal. He said that although—because of their humility—saints never show that they are aware of all that has to happen, they do have that knowledge. The Professor told me that Maharaj Ji's first child, a daughter, was born during the Great

Master's time. Maharaj Ji at that time was with the Great Master in Amritsar, where the latter had gone for treatment, when a telegram arrived from Pisawa, sent by Rao Sahib (Maharaj Ji's father-in-law). The telegram read, "Harjit blessed with a baby girl."

Bibi Lajjo, then in attendance on the Great Master, commented a little disappointedly on the child being a girl. But the Great Master remarked, "Don't worry, there will be boys also to follow."

All this took place on 24th October 1947. Then, when in April the Great Master passed away and Sardar Bahadur Ji came onto the 'gaddi', Beji came with Maharaj Ji's daughter and wife for his blessing and requested him to give the child a name. Sardar Bahadur Ji smiled and said, "Ask the father and mother to name her—they have been collecting names for months!" So Beji came to Sirsa and gave Sardar Bahadur Ji's message to Maharaj Ji.

Maharaj Ji was sitting in the kitchen at the time, having a meal with his sisters. He replied, "All right, let's all discuss it and name the child." Beji said that she thought there ought to be some ceremony, but Maharaj Ji replied, "Sardar Bahadur Ji's order is our ceremony." So the new-born baby was named Nirmaljeet.

Then Maharaj Ji jokingly said, "As we are all here, let's also name the two sons who will be coming."

Beji was surprised and asked, "How do you know that?"

Maharaj Ji replied, "The Great Master has already foretold them."

So Maharaj Ji also named them as Jasbir and Ranbir, saying, "We will call them Cuckoo and Rana." As we all know, Maharaj Ji has two sons who are called Cuckoo and Rana.

This incident is demonstrative that Maharaj Ji never believed in any kind of ceremonies or formalities, right from the beginning.

Great Master's illness

Once when talking about the Great Master, Maharaj Ji told us, "It was during the summer months and my father, who was at Sikanderpur, received a telegram from Dalhousie saying that the Great Master was seriously ill and that he should come immediately. So my father came to me at Sirsa, to catch a train from there, telling me that he was going to Dalhousie, giving the reason."

On hearing that the Great Master was seriously ill, Maharaj Ji got very upset and said, "I will come with you." But his father refused permission, saying, "You are not called, so I cannot take you."

Maharaj Ji then started weeping. His father consoled him saying, "Let me go and I will tell the Great Master that you want to come and if he agrees to it, then I will inform you."

When his father told the Great Master that

Charan was very upset and also wanted permission to come, the Great Master wrote him a letter, through his secretary, saying that he was feeling much better and would soon be normal and that if any such occasion arose in future, he would definitely call him.

Then, in the month of October, the Great Master again became very ill and was taken to Amritsar Satsang Ghar for treatment, and requested Lala Munshi Ram to ask Charan to join him there. When Maharaj Ji got the message, he said "I immediately handed over all my briefs to one of my colleagues and left the next morning for Beas, going directly from there to Amritsar. And I had the opportunity to stay with him for twenty days.

"Whilst I was there I received a letter from the Deputy Commissioner, Hissar, stating that my name had been forwarded for judicial services. So I took this letter to Maharaj Ji. He was lying down at the time, but at once sat up and very lovingly told me, 'Law practice and judicial service are not for you—I only wanted you to have experience of the courts. Now since your father is not in good health and cannot manage the farm, and with your younger brother being in the army, you should leave your law practice and join your father at the farm and look after it, relieving him of that burden.' And he sent me back to Sirsa the very next day."

After that, Maharaj Ji moved to the farm and started helping his father.

It so happened that about the third week of

December, Maharaj Ji again received a telegram
from the Dera, asking him to go to Delhi to receive
Dr. Schmidt—who had come from Geneva to
treat the Great Master—and bring him to Beas.
Maharaj Ji therefore immediately went to Delhi,
only to learn that Mr. Mehta had already taken
Dr. Schmidt to Beas. So he rushed to the Dera.
The Great Master kept him by his side throughout his illness, until he left the body, just as he
had promised. This was a little over three months
(December 25 to April 2).

Sardar Bahadur Ji's advice

Once during Sardar Bahadur Ji's time, Maharaj
Ji said he was very upset about some family problem and had made a very strong decision. Sardar
Bahadur Ji, who was at that time holding satsang
and initiation in Delhi, somehow came to know
about it. Maharaj Ji and his father were also with
him on that tour.

As everyone knows, Sardar Bahadur Ji was a
man of few words, so he told Maharaj Ji, who was
standing somewhere near, "Chowdhry, you should go
and do so and so." This was quite the opposite of
what Maharaj Ji had previously decided and he felt
it very difficult to reverse his decision. He was
taken aback and stood motionless without saying
anything, remaining there while Sardar Bahadur Ji
walked down to make the selection of a group who
were asking for initiation.

After half an hour, Sardar Bahadur Ji returned, finding Maharaj Ji still standing there, lost in himself. Sardar Bahadur Ji looked at him and, attracting his attention, said, "What can one not endure and go through in life, by keeping one's tongue between one's teeth!"[1]

Maharaj Ji told us, "I just bowed my head and quietly went away to obey him." Then he added, "I often found his advice to be very helpful and useful in dealing with so many of the situations which I have had to face."

A perfect disciple of a perfect Master.

Huzur Maharaj Ji's Inaugural Address

I was very fond of going to Professor Jagmohan Lal's house in the Dera and loved to hear from him all about Maharaj Ji, as he had been very close to the Great Master and had seen Maharaj Ji growing up from childhood, being groomed to be a Master. Maharaj Ji had also been the professor's student.

One day the professor told us about the inaugural address which Maharaj Ji gave on 4th November 1951. Professor Sahib was sitting with Maharaj Ji, when Babu Gulab Singh (an old satsangi) approached him and said, 'Since you are supposed to address the sangat tomorrow, I have written a speech for you to read to them.'

------

1. A Punjabi saying meaning 'by firm determination'.

INAUGURATION

"Maharaj Ji just thanked him and kept the paper. But I knew that Maharaj Ji would never read the speech. So I asked him, 'What have you in your mind to tell them?' He said, 'Professor Sahib, my heart bleeds, I wonder how it is going to express itself.'

"Then at the time of the pagri (inauguration) ceremony, Maharaj Ji gave an extemporaneous speech, without any notes or paper in his hands. His eyes were moist and his throat was choked and he was almost sobbing."

The following is a direct translation of his address. His emotion-laden and deeply moving words, full of love and humility, brought tears in the eyes of many present.

"My love for Huzur Maharaj Ji, the commands of Sardar Bahadur Maharaj Ji, and the affection of the sangat compel me to carry out the wishes of Sardar Bahadur Ji to serve the sangat and the Dera. But when I look at myself and my shortcomings, I feel diffident and find myself unable to decide whether I am really fit for these onerous duties. This struggle has prevented me so far from meeting the sangat, for which I ask your forgiveness.

"I wish to tell the sangat quite frankly that I do not make any claims whatsoever to spiritual attainments. I do not find in myself even those excellences that a good satsangi should possess.

"I had the good fortune of being at the feet of Huzur Maharaj Ji and of serving him during the last days of his illness, but Sardar Bahadur

Ji did not afford me even this privilege. I am so unlucky that I reached here only after his cremation and could not even have his last darshan.

"These orders were communicated to me by those fortunate devoted satsangis who were near Sardar Bahadur Ji, and I have no choice but to serve the Dera and the sangat according to his orders. I request the sangat to look upon me as their younger brother and thus help me in serving them and this great institution. If the sangat looks upon me in any other light, it would mean that you do not wish to support and cooperate with me, and that would be doing a great injustice to me.

"The passing away of Sardar Bahadur Ji has been a great shock to all of us. We had not yet got over the grief and sorrow caused by Huzur Maharaj Ji's departure when Sardar Bahadur Ji has also left us. Such personalities rarely come into this world. Only a great and highly advanced soul could lead such an immaculate, spotless life, free from all personal motives. We should not become dispirited nor feel helpless in this hour of our calamity, but should try to follow with confidence and firmness the path of Surat-Shabd Yoga pointed out to us by Huzur Maharaj Ji and Sardar Bahadur Ji. Huzur Maharaj Ji used to say that he is always with everyone. This assurance stands for all of us and not for me alone. I request all devoted sevadars of the Dera to faithfully carry out whatever duties he had entrusted to them.

"The sangat has assembled from far and near to do homage and pay their respects to Sardar Bahadur Maharaj Ji, and for this I thank you with all my heart.

"I repeat today before the entire sangat what I said yesterday to a group of devoted satsangis whom I had called for the purpose, namely, that I do not consider myself worthy of putting on the turban of such great saints. But, compelled by the sangat's love and faith in Huzur Maharaj Ji, I have submitted myself to the sangat, and the sangat can do as they see fit."

Maharaj Ji's grandmother

Talking about his grandmother (the Great Master's wife), Maharaj Ji said, "She was very much attached to me." While he was practising law at Sirsa, he was living there on his own for practically two years, and his grandmother often used to visit him, staying with him for several months at a stretch.

Every day, whatever Maharaj Ji earned as fees, he used to give to his grandmother, and she would tie the money in a corner of her 'chunni'.[1] After some time the whole 'chunni' was full of knots of money which Maharaj Ji had given to her—so she very innocently said, "Son,

----

1. A 'chunni' is a long scarf, made of a lightweight fabric and worn as a part of a lady's everyday Punjabi clothing.

my whole 'chunni' is full now, where will I keep
your money?"

Maharaj Ji laughed and said, "Maji, keep it
in the almirah or get another 'chunni'." He had
been very close to his grandmother. He said that
by nature she was a very simple and affectionate
lady.

***

It so happened, Maharaj Ji said, that when she
died she was at the Dera with the Great Master, but
no one else from the family was there. She left the
body just at the time when the Great Master was
about to go and hold satsang. He told Bibi Rali,
who was then in attendance, "We will cremate her
after satsang."

At this Bibi Rali was quite upset and said to
the Great Master, "How hard you are! My Mata Ji
has died and you are going to hold satsang."

But the Great Master just smiled and replied,
"She was Babaji's soul. He has taken her away:
now she no longer suffers," and saying this he
walked to satsang. After the satsang was over, he
announced to the sangat, "Your Mata Ji has died.
Now all of you should go and cremate her."

The next day Maharaj Ji, who was at Sirsa,
received a telegram sent from Lala Munshi Ram to
his father, which read, "Mata Ji died and cremated."

Maharaj Ji was very upset. Going to his father
at Sikanderpur, he showed him the telegram, saying,
"It is very unreasonable of the Great Master not
even to call us for her cremation. After all she was

your mother and our grandmother." But Maharaj Ji's father just said, "It is his mauj" and kept quiet. But Maharaj Ji still felt very hurt and without anyone's knowledge sent a telegram to his future father-in-law, Rao Sahib (he was engaged to be married in a few months), saying "Marriage postponed. Grandmother died."

After three days, the Great Master came to Sikanderpur, and naturally all the family members came to offer their condolences. Rao Sahib had also come and he gave Maharaj Ji's telegram to the Great Master. After reading it, the Great Master called Maharaj Ji and asked, "Was she nearer to you than to your father or to me?" Maharaj Ji kept quiet. Then the Great Master said, "One who has come has to go. She was Babaji's soul. He has taken her away. Why are you worried about her? Your marriage cannot be postponed." And so he was married as originally planned.

***

While Maharaj Ji was relating all this about his grandmother, Mr. R. N. Mehta from Delhi had also been sitting with us, and he told us that he had been at the Dera when Mata Ji died. He had come to the Dera with his wife and children for a week's visit. Every morning he would go and pay his respects to the Great Master and would also go along with him to visit Mata Ji, who was not well. He told us that three days before she died, she requested the Great Master to take her away, but the Great Master said, "Ask Babaji."

At this, Mata Ji got a little angry, saying "Babaji says I should ask you!"

Whereupon the Great Master smiled and replied, "What is the hurry? You have first to see the marriage of your grandson."

Then Mata Ji said, "I want to go. All my sons are settled, and my whole family is happy and flourishing. I want to leave now, I have no interest in anyone anymore."

So the Great Master replied, "All right, keep your attention inside and do dhyan of Babaji."

The next day when Mehta Sahib went with the Great Master to visit her, her attention was inside. The doctor who was attending her had procured some drugs from abroad for her treatment, hoping to help her get better. Those had just arrived, and standing with the box open, he asked the Great Master to bless them as he wanted to administer an injection. So the Great Master blessed them and permitted the doctor to give the injection.

But Mehta Sahib was puzzled and while walking with the Great Master to satsang, he asked him, "Why did you allow the doctor to prick her with his needles now?"

The Great Master replied, "Keep quiet! Let the Lord do His work and let the doctor do his work. She won't feel anything, and if I should tell the doctor not to give her the injection, when she passes away he would think that had they allowed him to give the injection, she might have been all right."

On the next day, Mehta Sahib went to take leave from the Great Master before returning to Rawalpindi. But the Great Master said, "First, please do something for me, but don't tell anyone about it. Tomorrow your Mata Ji will leave the body at 3.30 p.m. Please go to Lahore and bring Motia[1] along with other white flowers and garlands for her cremation."

So Mehta Sahib took his wife and children to Lahore. On reaching there, he told his wife, "You go on with the children to Rawalpindi. I have some work to do here for the Great Master and will follow you soon."

After he had seen his wife off at the station, he did as the Great Master had instructed him. He bought the flowers and kept them well covered in a basket.

He told me that he was then a new initiate of only a few years standing and was wondering whether what the Great Master had said would happen. He reached the Dera by the evening train, bringing the basket of flowers with him. At the station, a tonga was waiting for him. When he arrived at the Dera, he learnt that Mata Ji had died at 3.30 p.m. Mehta Sahib was wonderstruck and as a result of this incident was blessed with unshakable faith in his Master. He brought the flowers to the Great Master, bowed his head and gave them to him. Mata Ji was cremated that same evening.

---

1. Motia, a type of jasmine flower.

Great Master — last days

Talking about the Great Master's last days, Maharaj Ji said that he was called by the Great Master in December 1947, from Sikanderpur, and that he had stayed with the Great Master throughout his last illness. At that time, his younger brother Captain P. S. Grewal was in service with the army. Seeing the Great Master's condition in January, Maharaj Ji wrote to his brother, "The Great Master is becoming weaker and weaker every day. You should take leave and come, otherwise you will regret it for the rest of your life." It is evident that Maharaj Ji was conscious that the Great Master would soon be leaving.

His brother replied that he was making every effort, but that the authorities had refused him leave; however, he was still trying.

Maharaj Ji wrote back, "Even if you have to break your leg to resign from the army, it will be worth it. These are the days to serve and be near him. So do come." Somehow his brother managed to get leave, arriving ten days before the Great Master passed away. Maharaj Ji said, "He was a great moral support to me."

Dr. Schmidt had come from Geneva a few months before the Great Master left his body, to treat him during his last illness. Maharaj Ji told us, "One day the Great Master called me and said, 'After I leave you should take care of Dr. Schmidt, because everyone will forget about him. So you take him and show him whatever he wants to see and be with him till he leaves for his country. He has served me well with devotion and love. I am very pleased with him.' "

After the Great Master had expired, Maharaj Ji
asked Dr. Schmidt where he would like to go.
Dr. Schmidt said that he wanted to visit Simla and
Agra. So Maharaj Ji himself took him to those
places. In Agra, they stayed at the Dayal Bagh guest
house and met Mehta Sahib Ji Maharaj, who was
the guru there at that time. The management was
very kind and looked after them well. Maharaj Ji
also showed Soami Bagh to Dr. Schmidt, especially
the samadhi (mausoleum) of Soami Ji. Maharaj Ji
commented, "I can still remember Dr. Schmidt's
remark, 'How do you justify this in view of Soami
Ji's teachings?' But I did not answer him. I also
showed him all the other historical places in Agra."

Then Maharaj Ji took him to Delhi, where he
arranged for his stay at Maiden's Hotel. Maharaj Ji
himself paid all the expenses of the trip, not allow-
ing Dr. Schmidt to pay for anything. He then
saw him off safely to Bombay—where he was
to catch the plane for Geneva—having informed
the satsangis in Bombay that he was coming.
They also took very good care of him. Dr. Schmidt
wrote a letter of appreciation and gratitude to
Maharaj Ji; he said that he had been amazed to
see the love and devotion of satsangis everywhere. He wrote that they had all looked after him
extremely well, even though the Great Master had
not recovered and that if he had returned to health,
"I am sure that the satsangis would have weighed
me in gold!"

This incident demonstrates how Maharaj Ji
obeyed his Master's wishes explicitly, even to
the extent that when Dr. Schmidt visited India
several years later (after Maharaj Ji had become

the Master), he never allowed him even to pay for his shopping. I am reminded that when Maharaj Ji came to Indore for satsang, Dr. Schmidt accompanied him. At Indore when he wanted to buy some Indian caps which he liked, Maharaj Ji gave instructions, "Whatever he buys, do not take any money from him, but put it on my account."

***

Related to the above incident is another one which Maharaj Ji mentioned. He had been called to the Dera from the farm to be with the Great Master during his last few months. Maharaj Ji had brought only a few changes of clothes with him, not realizing how long he would be staying. One day, when he was leaving his house to go to the Great Master, his pyjama (Indian trousers) got caught on his foot and was torn. When he came before the Great Master, he saw the torn portion and said, "Don't you have any clothes?" Maharaj Ji just kept quiet.

Then the Great Master called Bibi Rali and said, "Go to the almirah. Bring the money you have kept tied in a handkerchief and give it to Charan. It is his money, which he has been giving to me." Bibi Rali brought the handkerchief and gave it to the Great Master, who then gave it to Maharaj Ji, telling him to have some clothes made.

Maharaj Ji told us that this was the surplus money that—whenever he visited the Dera—he would leave with Bibi Rali to give to the Great Master for covering his household expenses. Maharaj Ji did not know that the Great Master had

MAHARAJ JI AS A YOUNG LAWYER

not been using it, but had kept it all for him.
Maharaj Ji said that it had come in very handy
to cover all his expenses, when he had taken
Dr. Schmidt sightseeing to Simla and Agra. He had
borrowed a new Chevrolet car from Mr. R.C. Mehta
in which he had driven Dr. Schmidt on their tour to
Simla, Agra and Delhi, until he had put him on the
plane for Bombay.

The young lawyer

Today Beji (Maharaj Ji's mother) related something very interesting concerning Maharaj Ji's
younger days. He had just started his practice as a
lawyer. He had been the first Sikh lawyer to join
the bar, though there was a considerable Sikh population around Sirsa. During the first two or three
days an old man came to the court and said to the
other senior lawyers, "I would like to give my case
to the young lawyer who has just joined. Where
is he?"

The senior lawyers asked, "Why do you want to
engage him? He has just joined and has hardly had
any experience of conducting a case." But the old
man was adamant, saying that he only wanted the
young lawyer.

"Since he is so handsome," he pointed out,
"at least he will look dignified and graceful
while conducting my case." He said this because
Maharaj Ji used to dress well and looked elegant.
He was given the case and he won it. Thereafter,

he became a very popular lawyer and in great
demand.

Maharaj Ji's sense of humour

Once while we were with Beji, she mentioned
another very interesting incident concerning Maharaj
Ji. It always amazes me that at this age of over
ninety, how sharp is her memory. She said, "You
know that by nature Maharaj Ji is full of humour,
and enjoys making humorous remarks." One day he
was travelling by car with Sardar Bahadur Ji
Maharaj on a visit to Pathankot. During the return
drive, Sardar Bahadur Ji was sitting with Lala
Munshi Ram and Maharaj Ji on the back seat,
whilst Bhai Shadi, who was also with them, was
sitting on the front seat beside the driver. While they
were driving along, Maharaj Ji saw a 'naga sadhu'
riding on horseback, with his disciple following on
foot. The disciple could not keep pace with the
horse and was almost running. As it was summer,
the weather was very hot, and the road was burning
with heat. The poor disciple was sweating and his
feet were burning, as he had no shoes.

Seeing this scene, Maharaj Ji folded his hands
and bowed his head. Sardar Bahadur Ji noticed this
and asked smilingly, "Chowdhry, why did you do
that?"

At first Maharaj Ji kept quiet, but then, on the
insistence of Sardar Bahadur Ji, he said, "I was
thanking the Lord and was grateful to him that as a
disciple, he chose to give me Masters like you and

the Great Master. At least by your grace we wear
nice clothes and ride in a car with you. I was wondering how it would have been if the Lord had
made me a disciple of such a sadhu on horse back.
I shudder to think of my plight!" Hearing this,
Sardar Bahadur Ji (who also had a great sense of
humour) had a hearty laugh.

Great Master's last days

Today Maharaj Ji told us of a significant event
which took place during the Great Master's last
days. A devoted satsangi, Baba Karam Singh of
Jullundur, came to the Dera and reported to Bhai
Gandhi (a personal attendant of the Great Master)
that he had come to know from a confidential
source that one of the sevadarnis (lady sevadars) in
the Great Master's service had asked her brother to
draw up a document in which, as a reward for her
devoted service to the Great Master, he would give
Amritsar Satsang Ghar to her. Baba Karam Singh
told Bhai Gandhi, "This document is typed and
ready. It is in her possession, ready to be signed by
the Great Master. Please prevent it from being
signed."

So Bhai Gandhi approached Maharaj Ji, who
was here at that time in personal attendance on the
Great Master, and told him the whole story, asking
him to tell the Great Master and request him not to
sign.

Maharaj Ji replied, "How can I ask him that?
It is his property and if he wishes to give it away,

who am I to prevent it?" "Though," Maharaj Ji
added, "I thought that if really this is an attempt at
fraud, I must confirm it somehow or the other, and
if it is one, it should be stopped." At that time, they
all used to sleep in the Great Master's house. The
Great Master slept in the centre room, and on one
side in an adjoining room slept the ladies in attendance, while on the other side Maharaj Ji slept, in
the company with a few men.

By nightfall, everyone was dead tired and in
deep sleep. Maharaj Ji quietly went to where the
ladies were sleeping and gently extracted the particular paper from out of her pocket. Reading it, he
found that all he had been told was absolutely true,
and that the paper had not yet been signed by the
Great Master. Maharaj Ji then quietly slipped the
paper back into the lady's pocket.

He told us that after this he was rather miserable, because he could find no solution to the problem. The same question came to his mind again and
again. "If the Great Master really wants to give her
the satsang ghar because she has served him for so
many years, then who am I to question it? But if
his signature is going to be obtained by fraud, by
spinning out some long tale, then it should be
stopped at any cost." It worried him considerably.
So he went for a walk to the riverside to think over
the problem, but came back without finding any
solution.

On his return, he went with Dr. Schmidt to the
Great Master. Then, without his asking, the Great
Master gave Maharaj Ji his pen, telling him that the
pen kept on slipping down from under his pillow,
hurting his back, making him very uncomfortable.

"So," the Great Master said, "you keep it. Whenever I need it to sign anything, I will call you." Maharaj Ji was so relieved and bowed his head silently in gratitude, thinking, "How, without my saying anything, he has solved my problem."

***

The pen remained with Maharaj Ji at all times, and in this context, Maharaj Ji narrated another incident. Lala Munshi Ram was the Great Master's secretary. He was a wise and shrewd man, though absolutely unassuming. All the Dera funds and everything in Dera legally belonged to the Great Master, and the Dera bank account was in his personal name. As the will had already been made by the Great Master, appointing Sardar Bahadur Ji as his successor, Lala Munshi Ram realized that after the Great Master would leave the body, a great deal of Dera money would be spent in going to probate to transfer the account to Sardar Bahadur Ji's name. So he thought it best to open a joint account in the names of Sardar Bahadur Ji, the Great Master and himself, and transfer some funds to this account.

Consequently, he made out a cheque and asked the Great Master to sign it. The Great Master did not want to hurt him by refusing, and as Maharaj Ji was not available at that moment, he signed the cheque in a slightly different way from his usual signature. Lala Munshi Ram took the cheque to the bank, but as the signatures did not tally, the manager refused to honour it, saying, "I am sorry, but the signatures are different, and since the amount is very large, could you please bring another cheque?"

Lala Munshi Ram returned to the Dera at lunch time in a worried state of mind. He told Maharaj Ji what had happened at the bank, saying, "The Great Master's hand has become shaky and he is unable to sign his correct signature any more. I do not know what to do."

Maharaj Ji just said, "Let me have a new cheque. I will get it signed again."

So Maharaj Ji took the cheque to the Great Master, gave him his pen and explained about the transfer of the money. The Great Master signed the cheque, using his normal signature. Then Maharaj Ji gave the cheque to Lala Munshi Ram with a smile.

Lala Munshi Ram

Once, talking about Lala Munshi Ram's loyalty to the institution and his honesty in dealing with the Dera money, Maharaj Ji related an incident which had taken place during his first satsang tour, after he had come to the 'gaddi'.

He was going to Dehra Dun, accompanied by Lala Munshi Ram and Mr. Ahluwalia. Dr. Stone and Miss Hilger were also with him. Lala Munshi Ram had been secretary to the Great Master, to Sardar Bahadur Ji and then to Maharaj Ji. At that time, Mr. Ahluwalia had just joined and was under training.

Lala Munshi Ram gave Mr. Ahluwalia some money for the tour expenses—for train tickets, tonga fare and so on. Then, in the evening, he asked Mr. Ahluwalia to give him an account of the expenditure. Mr. Ahluwalia tried to remember whatever had been spent during the course of the journey and submitted it. But the account fell short by twenty rupees. So Lala Munshi Ram asked Mr. Ahluwalia to replace the twenty rupees from his own pocket, saying, "This is Dera money and if you forget what it was spent on, then you have to pay! In future, I would advise you to keep a diary and write down every amount before giving it to anyone. Every paisa should be accounted for, because it is the sangat's hard-earned money and their seva."

Maharaj Ji added later, "Babaji was also very particular in keeping account even of a paisa. Each and every item of expenditure which was incurred during his time at the Dera is mentioned in his diaries."

Related to this, Maharaj Ji continued with another interesting story. Because this satsang tour was his first one, he had no experience of what might be needed and he assumed that cooking and serving utensils would be provided wherever the arrangements for their stay were made. But when Maharaj Ji and his party sat down for lunch, their food was served in silver dishes. Maharaj Ji was surprised and felt embarrassed and asked Lala Munshi Ram, "What is this?"

Lala Munshi Ram replied, "If you do not bring your own utensils with you, this is what is going to happen. On this occasion it is silver, but the next time it will be gold, and so it will go on."

Then Maharaj Ji immediately called his servant and told him that as soon as they reached Delhi, he should buy whatever utensils and crockery were needed for cooking and serving, telling him that he should always take those things with him whenever they went on tour. "After that," Maharaj Ji said, "whatever I needed personally was always carried by my servant, including the rations. Whatever vege-tables, milk and other eatables were bought on our behalf, were always paid for."

***

Then Maharaj Ji told us another interesting incident concerning Lala Munshi Ram, as to how wise and astute he was. Maharaj Ji greatly admired him for his wisdom, especially in his handling of the Dera finances.

Maharaj Ji once accompanied Lala Munshi Ram to Delhi. Mr. Mehta had bought some land by collecting funds from the satsangis. When Maharaj Ji came to know about it, he decided to return the money to the satsangis and buy the land out of Dera money. So Maharaj Ji, along with Lala Munshi Ram, first went to Jullundur to get the money from the bank. It was quite a large amount, about three hundred thousand rupees, and Lala Munshi Ram had a particular canvas bag which he always used for carrying money.

Maharaj Ji and he boarded the train at Jullun-dur—the Flying Mail—bound for Delhi. They had a coupe[1] to themselves. Lala Munshi Ram handed the bag to Maharaj Ji saying, "You take care of it. I am old and may fall asleep. You are younger and can

1. A compartment containing two bunks.

take better care of it." He then retired to the upper bunk and fell fast asleep.

Throughout the journey, Maharaj Ji sat holding the bag tightly under his thigh, without blinking an eyelid. Mr. Mehta was at the station to receive them at Delhi, and took them to Darya Ganj where Maharaj Ji was to stay. On reaching there, Lala Munshi Ram gave the canvas bag to Mr. Bhargawa of Delhi, to be kept in his safe.

The next morning, at about 8 a.m. Mr. Mehta collected together all the satsangis who were to receive their money back. Then Lala Munshi Ram asked for Mr. Bhargawa, in order to have the bag returned to him. But he was told that Mr. Bhargawa had left for a court case early in the morning, and no one knew when he would return.

Maharaj Ji then asked Lala Munshi Ram, "What should be done now?"

But Lala Munshi Ram said, "Do not worry. Come with me." And he took Maharaj Ji into another room and told him, "Actually, the money is in my inside pocket. It is not in the bag."

Upon hearing this Maharaj Ji was surprised and said, "But you made me hold the bag throughout the journey from Jullundur to Delhi when there was no money in it! Why?"

He replied, "I had to do it. This is the sangat's money, belonging to the Dera. Everyone could see us going to the bank and coming out. So if some thief had wanted to rob us, he would have snatched the bag. He would never have thought that the money was with me. I have to take precautions." Upon hearing this, Maharaj Ji felt deeply impressed by his logic and the care and loyalty which he had for the institution.

Lala Munshi Ram also added, "Even when I take the seva money from the Dera to deposit in the State Bank in Amritsar, I do the same thing. Giani Karam Singh holds the bag, a Dera chowkidar (watchman) with a gun in his hand follows him to guard the bag, and I walk behind them leisurely with the money in my inside pocket! So if anybody snatches the bag, then the guard will shoot at the person and even if the thief does get away with the bag, he will get nothing.

"When I reach the bank, I take the bag from Giani Karam Singh again. And so far, nobody has even suspected that the bag does not contain any money, and that it has some old books which I carry in my hand when I come out of the Bank."

"There was such loyalty, honesty and wisdom in Lala Munshi Ram," Maharaj Ji said, "I had the deepest regard for him."

Babaji's letters

Once, talking about the Great Master's last days, Maharaj Ji said, "A couple of days before the Great Master wrote his will, he called Bhai Bhan Singh and asked him to recite the shabd of Soami Ji Maharaj, 'Oh Brother, turn thou homeward now, you are a stranger in a foreign land.'

"Dr. Schmidt, Dr. Hazara Singh and I were sitting there. The Great Master just closed his eyes, and after that he did not talk to anyone for half an hour or so. Then he asked me to call Bibi Rali. On her arrival, he asked for Babaji's letters. Bhua Ji brought a beautiful blue velvet-covered box containing the letters. They were always kept in the almirah by the side of the Great Master's bed. The Great Master first put the box to his forehead and after opening it, took out one letter, kissed it, and put on his glasses, holding the letter in both his hands. He read it for about fifteen minutes. His eyes were moist. Then he put that letter back in the same box once more. After closing it, he again put it to his forehead and asked me to keep it with me, to keep it in the family. He said, 'This is my personal treasure.' Then he closed his eyes. I was just wonderstruck and my throat was so choked that I could not say anything. Apart from myself, only Dr. Schmidt and Dr. Hazara Singh were present.

"Meanwhile, Bhua Rali came back into the room, and not knowing of the Great Master's instructions to me, she took the precious box away from me and put it back in the almirah. I could not say anything to her and just kept quiet. But it always haunted me, even after the Great Master's death, that the Great Master had given me personal responsibility of taking care of the box.

"Then, during Sardar Bahadur Ji's time, when I first came to the Dera, he at once asked Bibi Rali to get the box containing Babaji's letters and handed it over to me saying, 'This is your family property, the Great Master entrusted this to you.'

"With tears in my eyes I told him, 'You are the

head of our family now; you are the right person to keep it.'

"He looked at me very lovingly, just nodded his head, and put it in the same place saying, 'You can collect it from here whenever you need it.'

"After I came to the Dera, that was the first thing I took care of, and due to the insistence of Miss Hilger, a few portions of those letters were translated into English by Professor Jagmohan Lal. She took the notes, typed them, and the Dera published them under the title of *Spiritual Letters*."

Lala Munshi Ram's loyalty to the Dera

One day, Maharaj Ji was reminiscing to a few Dera officials about Lala Munshi Ram. He said that during Sardar Bahadur Ji's time, a joint account had been opened in the names of Sardar Bahadur Ji and Lala Munshi Ram. Then, a few months after Maharaj Ji had come to the 'gaddi', Master Uday Singh—an old and devoted satsangi who used to keep the Dera accounts—approached Maharaj Ji and asked if he knew of an account held with the State Bank at Ambala, in the names of Sardar Bahadur Ji and Lala Munshi Ram.

Maharaj Ji told him that he did not know about it. Master Uday Singh said that since Sardar Bahadur Ji was no more, the account would presently be in the sole name of Lala Munshi Ram. So he suggested that Maharaj Ji should ask Lala Munshi Ram to have it transferred. Professor

Jagmohan Lal also advised Maharaj Ji similarly. He said that if Maharaj Ji did not talk to Lala Munshi Ram, then he would. "After all," the Professor said, "it is Dera money. If it remains in Munshi Ram's name and he happens to die suddenly, it will naturally be inherited by his son."

But Maharaj Ji said, "Please do not say anything to Munshi Ram Ji. If he has not told me, he must have some very good reason. I have full faith in his honesty and integrity."

Time passed and Maharaj Ji never broached this subject to Munshi Ram. Then another old devoted satsangi of the Great Master, a retired district and sessions judge, Lala Gulwant Rai, told Maharaj Ji that he knew that the Great Master had left eight lakhs (eight hundred thousand) rupees, yet in the Dera account there were only three lakhs. So the remaining five lakhs must be in the Ambala State Bank. He suggested that Maharaj Ji have a talk with Lala Munshi Ram.

But again, Maharaj Ji presented the same argument, requesting Lala Gulwant Rai not even to let Lala Munshi Ram know that Maharaj Ji knew of the account.

After a few months, Lala Munshi Ram came to Maharaj Ji's house one afternoon. He was considerably worried, saying, "I could not sleep last night due to a pain in my chest."

Naturally, Maharaj Ji was concerned and suggested that he should consult a doctor in Amritsar. Lala Munshi Ram said, "I will be all right, but I have been worrying all night that there is an account held in my name only, at the Ambala State bank—

and it is Dera money. I had not told you about it, because—to tell the truth—I was not sure how you would handle the Dera funds, being so young. But now I would like this amount to be transferred to your name."

Maharaj Ji laughed and said, "Are you sure you can trust me now? I am still young!"

Then Munshi Ram Ji said, "I have seen you working and administering the Dera. You have no interest in money or accounts. You are completely detached. I am sorry I did not tell you earlier. Let us go to Ambala and do the needful; then only will my mind be at ease."

So, they went to Ambala and there, at the State Bank, they met Mr. Ahluwalia's son, who was the manager. He told them that his father was at his home, and had invited everyone for lunch. So Maharaj Ji and Lala Munshi Ram had lunch with them. While they were there, Lala Munshi Ram requested Mr. R.D. Ahluwalia to come to the Dera to help him with the administration, as he was getting old and could not handle everything alone. In due course of time, Mr. Ahluwalia joined the Dera service.

Tradition of the Masters

Talking about the Great Master, Maharaj Ji once said in satsang that all his life the Great Master had been very particular not to use anything given to him, without payment. One day, a few months before leaving his body, the Great Master announced after satsang, "I have never used Dera funds for my personal use. I have lived within my own income. Sometimes, Bibi Rali might have taken some vegetables grown in the Dera garden and cooked them for me, and I have also used the Dera car for satsang purposes. For these, I ask the sangat's forgiveness. If anyone owes me any money, I absolve him of that. If I owe anything to anybody, I request him to take the payment from me."

Maharaj Ji also said that when the Great Master was in army service, the orderly in his office once entrusted him with forty rupees, to keep on his behalf. But then he went on leave to his village and never came back. The Great Master tried to trace his relatives in order to return the money, but he could not locate them.

Then, a few months before the Great Master was to leave his body, he called one of the sevadars, Gopal Singh Latha, and gave him forty rupees to deposit in seva.

***

Maharaj Ji has also maintained the same high tradition, established by all saints and has lived on his own personal resources, supporting his family and children on the income from his farm. Bibi Rali used to tell us that even as a very young boy, he never asked for anything from anyone, not even from his own elders in the family. Even if one of his family members or friends took something belonging to him, he could not ask him to give it back.

Once, referring to this noble tradition of the saints, Maharaj Ji said in satsang, "I would like to request the sangat not to give any money or any gift to any of my relatives or my family members, even if they ask for it or need it. Even if I were to ask for anything, please refuse me. The Great Master has left enough to look after us."

The saints are themselves living examples of the high ideals that they preach.

Happiness lies in contentment

Maharaj Ji once said in satsang that in this modern age people have become quite self-centred. They have forgotten how to relax, and families are drifting apart. In olden days, all the younger ones looked up to the family elders for advice. They gave them respect and they all sat together regularly. Now, no one tolerates anyone else, and there is no happiness and contentment despite so much material gain.

To illustrate this point, Maharaj Ji mentioned that the Great Master once went to the farm at Sikanderpur at a time when construction work was going on. In the evening, the whole family sat around him. His eldest son, Sardar Bachint Singh, had also come from his nearby farm and he began telling the Great Master his problems concerning the family and the farm. The Great Master, however, did not pay any attention to him, for he was listening to the labourers who were singing folk songs together, after their day's work. They were laughing and dancing and singing, and the Great Master was enjoying their simple happiness.

Sardar Bachint Singh again tried to draw the Great Master's attention to his problems. Then the Great Master said, "Just look at these labourers—they earn only eight annas (half a rupee) a day—but they have no complaints. How happy and contented they are! I have given you so much property and wealth, but still you come to me only with your problems."

Sardar Bachint Singh said, "But how can you compare grape vines with wild berries?"

The Great Master replied, "You are not happy and contented even with grapes, while they are happy and contented to eat wild berries. Happiness does not lie in wealth and property, but in contentment."

Maharaj Ji concluded, "These were the simple truths that the Great Master used to convey to us in just a few words. But they were great things to learn."

———

Dera's first well

Another incident, often narrated by Maharaj Ji, is how the Great Master received permission from Babaji to build a well at the Dera. It was during Babaji's time that the Great Master first visited the Dera. To begin with he was new to the place and knew nothing about it. In the morning, Bibi Rukko, who was in attendance on Babaji, asked the Great Master, "May I bring water for your bath?"

The Great Master naturally thought that she would bring the water from river Beas, which used to flow close by in those days. But when the water was brought, the Great Master was surprised to see that it was pure and clean. He thought, "This cannot be river water." So he asked her, "From where did you bring it?"

She replied, "From a well in the village Waraich," which was quite some distance away. Then the Great Master felt very embarrassed that she had to bring water for him all the way from the village.

The next morning, he requested her, "If you permit me, I would like to bring water from the village for Babaji's bath." But the Great Master had not been used to carrying anything heavy while he was in service, nor had he done any manual work in his life. He had been an engineer in the military service. So when he went to the village and put the pitcher of water on his head, he found it very heavy, and it was with great difficulty that he brought it to the Dera.

On his way back, he thought that there should be a well at the Dera for the use of Babaji and the sangat. So the Great Master hesitatingly asked Babaji, "If you permit me, I would like to get a well dug here, so that Bibi does not have to go all the way to the village for water. Besides, so many people come here and they could also make use of it."

At first Babaji refused, saying, "I am a sadhu. Today I am here, tomorrow if I do not like the place, I may go somewhere else. I do not want to build anything that will bind me to this place."

Once again the Great Master requested, "I do not want to bind you. I will be very happy if you drink water from the well just once. You may go wherever you please. I do not want to bind you."

Babaji loved the Great Master immensely, so he said, "All right, I will not be bound, but you will be bound to this place." So the excavation of the well began, and a major portion of the money for its construction was sent by the Great Master. Then, later, the Great Master realized just what Babaji's words had meant.

Babaji's first visit to Mehmansinghwala

Soon after his initiation, the Great Master requested Babaji to visit his village, Mehmansinghwala, and to hold satsang there. Babaji agreed, but the Great Master wanted Babaji to give satsang from the Adi Granth, because the words 'Radha Soami' and 'Sar Bachan' were not familiar to the Punjabi people.

In the satsang, Babaji took a shabd from the Adi Granth. Bibi Rukko, who was then in attendance on Babaji, went up onto the roof-terrace of the Great Master's house in the evening and began singing shabds in her powerful voice, from the *Sar Bachan*, in praise of Radha Soami. The Great Master always used to say that on hearing her, all his concern over public opinion vanished from his mind.

The first visit of Babaji Maharaj to Mehmansinghwala was a great occasion for the Great

Master. Babaji stayed with him, and the Great Master personally looked after all his needs. He drew water from the well for Babaji's bath, ground the wheat into flour and did the smallest chores with great love. One of the Great Master's daughters-in-law, seeing him do all this, offered to do it herself, saying, "This service is for us ladies."

The Great Master gently refused, saying, "This is my seva, I will do it."

Sardar Bahadur Ji — the living example

Sardar Bahadur Ji was also a living example of how a true satsangi should live in the world. He did not involve himself in worldly affairs at all. He never carried a penny with him, and used to give his entire salary to his friend, Pandit Lal Chand, who was often found to be staying with him. Out of this money he used to take care of Sardar Bahadur Ji's household expenses, his clothes or whatever else was needed. After these expenses had been met, the balance was sent to Sardar Bahadur's brother, Sardar Bhagat Singh.

Masters never forsake their disciples

Maharaj Ji often mentioned that even if an initiate goes off the path, the Master never leaves him, but takes care of him at the time of his death, though such disciples do have to pay for their bad karmas.

As an example, he said that once there was a truly devoted satsangi of the Great Master who had a very large family—about nine children. Then his wife died, leaving all these children behind for him to look after.

The Great Master visited him to offer his condolences, consoling him by saying that these are just karmic associations which we have with one another. When they are over, then the soul leaves the body. "So do not worry," he said, "and have courage."

But the satsangi was so depressed and so beside himself with grief, that he said to the Great Master, "If we have to pay for our karmas, then what is the purpose of having a Master like you?" The Great Master kept quiet, and came back to the Dera.

As time passed, the satsangi went astray from the path. He started drinking and eating meat. He also married again—a girl much younger in age. Though he used to attend satsang sometimes and always spoke about Sant Mat and the Great Master with devotion, he did not relinquish his bad habits. He never again came to the Dera.

After the Great Master and Sardar Bahadur Ji departed from this world, the present Master came onto the 'gaddi'. Then, whilst on a satsang tour to Simla, some satsangis approached Maharaj Ji and told him that this satsangi wanted to see him personally. Maharaj Ji had known him since childhood—having seen him with the Great Master

—so naturally out of respect and kindness, he went to meet him.

The man talked to Maharaj Ji about the Great Master with great love and devotion, but did not say anything about his habits. Maharaj Ji also did not mention anything about them, so as not to make him conscious of his weaknesses, so that he might not avoid him altogether. Maharaj Ji just advised him to give some time to meditation every day.

A year later, on his next tour to Simla, the satsangi again met Maharaj Ji, this time telling him his entire life story; what he had said to the Great Master, how he had gone off the path, and all that he had done. He said, "One day the Great Master appeared in meditation and I asked if he would take care of me at death."

The Great Master replied that he would definitely be taken care of, but that he would have to suffer very heavily and would have to pay off the karmas in this very life.

So he asked Maharaj Ji, "I knew I would have to suffer. I only request you that the time should be shortened."

Maharaj Ji replied, "The Great Master knows best. You should put your request to him."

Maharaj Ji said that when the end came, he did suffer a lot. His legs were amputated due to gangrene, and he died within a few days of entering the hospital. He was also all alone at the time and not even one of his nine children was near him.

Once initiated, Masters never abandon a soul.

The Dera Trust

It had been an accepted principle since Babaji's time that the Satguru was the sole and absolute owner of all the satsang property, as well as of any funds and of whatever seva in kind was offered by the disciples. The Great Master inherited this principle and so did Sardar Bahadur Ji and Maharaj Ji.

But Maharaj Ji could foresee the difficulties which could arise from this procedure due to the changing laws of the country and the new taxes being imposed upon land and income. In fact, by the time Maharaj Ji came here as the Master, a law had already been introduced by the government, restricting an individual to a maximum holding—in his personal name—of only thirty acres of land.

So, around 1957, Maharaj Ji told Lala Munshi Ram that he would like to create a Trust Society and would like to transfer all the Dera funds and the ownership of all the satsang property to this Society. Lala Munshi Ram opposed the suggestion and so did Professor Jagmohan Lal, saying, "This is against the basic tenets of Sant Mat. The Satguru is the sole owner. If we do this, the whole concept will be changed. This should not be done."

Maharaj Ji pleaded, "I can hold only thirty acres of land as an individual. So how can I hold land at Sikanderpur and also at the Dera?"

"But," they insisted, "the Dera is your spiritual inheritance, and Sikanderpur is your personal inheritance." In fact, they had already made a petition to the court and won the case. So Maharaj Ji was permitted to own his spiritual inheritance at the

Dera, as well as thirty acres at Sikanderpur, to provide for his personal income.

Then, during that year, Rai Sahib Lala Tarachand Agarwal, who was Deputy Custodian General for the Government of India, was initiated. Maharaj Ji consulted him about creating a Trust Society for the Dera. Tarachand Ji could see Maharaj Ji's point of view and agreed to form a Society of which Maharaj Ji would be the Patron. He also helped to convince Lala Munshi Ram and Professor Jagmohan Lal, pointing out that seva could still be offered to Maharaj Ji, but he would receive it as the Patron and then give it to the Trust. Then the funds would be used for the development of the Dera, by approval of the Society members.

Again, Lala Munshi Ram advised Maharaj Ji, "With this proposal the members will give you a lot of trouble. Since they will have power, they will not work according to your wishes."

Maharaj Ji replied, "Do not worry. If they will not go along with me, I will go along with them. They will not give me any trouble."

So, very reluctantly, Lala Munshi Ram and Professor Jagmohan Lal agreed. Then Lala Munshi Ram said, "I am getting old. It will not be possible for me to keep complicated accounts. I have always kept only one register since the Great Master's time, in which I write the expenditure on one side, and on the other side, I record whatever is credited." But by then, Mr. Ahluwalia had joined the Dera service, and he offered to keep the Trust account. As is often the case with the Masters, things worked out perfectly, though the evidence of their wisdom may be seen by us only with hindsight.

Hence, with the help of Lala Tarachand, the Trust was formed just at the right time. Indeed, with Maharaj Ji himself being a lawyer, most of the rules and regulations of Radha Soami Satsang Beas were drafted by him. Thus it was only by the great foresight of Maharaj Ji that the Dera was saved from considerable taxes and complications.

During the period when all this was going on, Maharaj Ji also wrote a letter to Lala Munshi Ram, who was then the Secretary, asking him how much cash the Dera was holding and also to provide him with a list of all the satsang ghars in India belonging to the Dera.

Lala Munshi Ram provided this information. Then Maharaj Ji wrote to him to transfer ownership of all the cash and the satsang ghars to Radha Soami Satsang Beas, and Lala Munshi Ram did the needful. The record of all this correspondence is presently kept in the Secretariat.

Eye Camp

While on tour among the villages in rural and mountainous areas, Maharaj Ji used to notice how a large number of people suffered from cataract and other eye diseases. Maharaj Ji felt compassion for these people, for he knew that the majority of them would be unable to afford or even find the necessary medical attention. In view of this, he decided to open an eye camp at the Dera where free operations and follow-up treatment could be provided by experts.

The first Dera eye camp was held in February, 1965. Eye specialists from Sitapur Eye Hospital near Aligarh in Uttar Pradesh—consisting of Dr. J. M. Pahwa and his team—came at the Dera's invitation and treated about two thousand patients, free of charge. All the nine hundred and fifty major operations and the three hundred minor ones which they performed were successful.

Since then, with the number of both patients and sevadars increasing steadily, the eye camp has become an annual feature of Dera life, providing a wonderful opportunity for seva. Satsangi doctors from all over India and abroad come to the Dera to serve in the eye camp. Many educated satsangis from other professions—lawyers, government officials, businessmen and so on—also come to the Dera in a spirit of loving devotion, to perform various tasks not requiring medical expertise.

The eye camp is open to all and no distinction is made between satsangi and non-satsangi patients. They are not even asked whether they are initiates or not. Each patient is provided with food, bed, clean linen, medicines, all the necessary medical tests and spectacles—all absolutely free of charge. Maharaj Ji himself visits the eye camp two or three times every day. His grace and mercy and, above all, his loving concern for the patients—the majority of whom are non-satsangis—inspire the sangat to serve and lovingly care for each and every patient in a spirit of selfless dedication.

Today in November 1989, it is twenty-four years since the first eye camp was held—this being the twenty-second eye camp. The progress and improvement in running the camps over the years is phenomenal. Dr. J. M. Pahwa and his team still perform the operations every year. This year nearly eleven thousand patients were screened, and just under six thousand were accepted as suitable for operation after final screening. Nearly five thousand three hundred of them were cataract patients, and the remainder were for glaucoma, optical iridectomy and other ailments.

There were thirty-five wards for males and sixty for females. Lady volunteers undertook the preparation of eye-pads and bandages, as well as the masks and caps worn by the medical staff. In all, about seven thousand sevadars served the patients and helped in the administrative work with total dedication.

There were two hundred and thirty-two doctors from all parts of India and other countries, including twenty-one from abroad. There were two hundred and eighty-six nurses, thirty-seven laboratory technicians, seventy-one pharmacists and fourteen operating theatre technicians. All of them rendered seva with love and selfless devotion.

The guiding and inspiring spirit for this stupendous task is Maharaj Ji. Out of his overflowing and benign grace and his keen interest in the welfare of the patients, Maharaj Ji spent over one and a half hours on November 3rd, visiting the screening venue, the operating theatre, the wards, the stores, etc. He went on foot and, as the days passed, he took frequent rounds of the wards where patients were kept after their operations.

His visits were a source of joy and inspiration

to professionals and lay sevadars alike, while his grace provided a healing touch to the sick and the deprived.

Representatives from the All India Radio and the Television Department of the Government of India covered the function, broadcasting and telecasting reports on the 3rd and the 11th, respectively, presenting some interesting cameos of all that was taking place.

Since 1965, 137,935 cases have been screened and 58,971 patients have undergone operations, restoring their sight. This gives one an idea of the scale of the work undertaken.

Below are two touching and beautiful speeches given by Maharaj Ji in praise of the service which the sevadars perform so lovingly. On November 20th, 1985, addressing the eye camp sevadars who had assembled in the grounds of the Satsang Ghar to receive parshad, Maharaj Ji spoke these inspiring words:

"Huzur Maharaj Ji (the Great Master) used to say that blessed are those who get the opportunity of serving others. It is the infinite grace of the Lord that the eye patients have given the sangat the privilege of serving them. There is no parallel in the world for the love and devotion with which you have all served the patients, performing the most arduous duties, unmindful of your comfort and convenience. I do not have words to express my feelings of appreciation. All that I can do is to pray to Huzur Maharaj Ji that he may bestow his grace on all of us."

On a similar occasion, he spoke almost the same words, adding, "We are grateful to the eye patients who have given us this opportunity to serve them."

Again, on November 22nd, 1987 Maharaj Ji addressed the eye camp sevadars as follows, after giving them parshad. He said:

"The foundation of this Dera was laid by Babaji Maharaj and Shri Huzur Maharaj Ji only on love, seva, humility and meditation. In this Dera all are equal—rich and poor, women and men, of any race or religion. There is no question of caste or creed. This Dera belongs to all, to every satsangi.

"The love with which the sangat serves the eye patients is but a noble example of these principles. The love and devotion with which you have served the eye patients this year and have served them every year—I am not exaggerating—has hardly a parallel in the world. I am not used to making long speeches. I am only used to folding my hands (in obeisance) before Huzur Maharaj Ji.

"Now, too, I fold my hands before him to beg that he continues to bless his sevadars to serve the eye patients, as in previous years, and likewise to shower his grace on me and his sangat."

This moving speech had an indescribable impact on the sevadars, many of whom broke down, overwhelmed with emotion.

Construction and opening of Maharaj
Sawan Singh Charitable Hospital, Beas

Although many people have been treated in the eye camps since 1965, for one reason or another a considerable number of those who came could not be admitted for eye surgery and had to return to their homes. Many of these people were desperately poor and could not afford to go to a hospital in the cities. Maharaj Ji was aware of this and knew that they would never receive treatment; and this used to pain him.

Thinking this over, Maharaj Ji considered the feasibility of building a permanent charitable hospital, where these poor people could be treated all the year round.

When he put the idea before the Dera staff members, they were surprised and reluctant to accept it, saying that they had hardly any funds for such a huge project, and that running it alone would cost a great deal of money. But Maharaj Ji had already decided to build the hospital, to give relief to the poor suffering humanity, and to take care of the sangat. So he told them, "Do not worry, the Great Master will take care of everything." Maharaj Ji told them that it would be called the Maharaj Sawan Singh Charitable Hospital.

The land was acquired from the military department and from the Punjab Government, at a reasonable price. In fact, the government wanted to give it free, but Maharaj Ji insisted on paying fully, whatever was the cost.

When digging of the foundation was ready to

MAHARAJ SAWAN SINGH CHARITABLE HOSPITAL — UNDER CONSTRUCTION

MAHARAJ SAWAN SINGH CHARITABLE HOSPITAL, BEAS

begin, Maharaj Ji just took a few staff members with him, without telling them anything. He had also previously asked some sevadars from Babaji's village of Ghoman to be at the site. Maharaj Ji asked them to pray to the Great Master and start the work. He made no ceremony of it.

Thus began the construction of the hospital and many thousands of sevadars, off and on, coming from all over India, helped to build it with great love and dedication and in whatever capacity they could serve.

It was completed in January 1986. The day before its official opening, Maharaj Ji held satsang there, at the beginning of which he addressed the sangat in the following words:

"Before starting the satsang I should like to mention that with the infinite grace of Huzur Maharaj Ji, the construction of the hospital building has been completed. At 9 o'clock tomorrow morning the OPD (Out Patients Department) of the hospital will be opened for patients. Thereafter, the OPD will remain open daily for patients, from 8 a.m. to 1 p.m. and 2 p.m. to 5 p.m. All patients, without any distinction between satsangis and non-satsangis, will be treated free of charge. Gradually, the hospital will begin to cater for indoor patients, for whom 300 beds have been provided.

"The construction and equipment of the hospital have cost us nine crores (ninety million) of rupees. The love and devotion with which the sangat has helped in the construction of the hospital has no parallel anywhere in the

world, nor do I have adequate words to express
my appreciation and gratitude for the same. The
local sangat as well as the satsangis living
abroad have contributed generously to the construction of and the equipment for the hospital.
With the infinite grace of Huzur Maharaj Ji, the
sangat has been afforded the opportunity of
serving the patients with the same love and
devotion.

"The sangat has also contributed liberally to
the building of a fund sufficient for running the
hospital, and a Trust has been created for the
managing and running of the hospital on the
interest from the Trust Fund.

"I should also like to assure the hospital
staff that the management will attend to all
their essential needs, but it is incumbent on
them to remember that they should serve the
patients with all the care and attention that
they need, and thereby enhance the glory of
the Great Master, whose name the hospital
bears, and in whose memory it has been
built with such rare love and devotion of the
sangat."

The hospital has now been running for
practically four years, serving thousands of
patients who would otherwise have had nowhere
else to go and no one to take care of them.
This is all due to the grace of Maharaj Ji and
the thoughtfulness and kindness that he has for
the suffering humanity.

RAVINES BEING FILLED FOR EXTENSION OF LANGAR

Dera

To impress upon the sangat that the Dera should always remain a spiritual centre only, as were Babaji's wishes when he chose this deserted place for meditation and for holding satsang, Maharaj Ji once addressed the sangat:

"Before starting the satsang I would like to make an important submission to the sangat. Please listen attentively, and try to understand what I am saying.

The Site

"Whenever saints want to select a permanent place of stay, they look for a quiet and secluded spot. They always prefer to remain aloof from the commotion of villages and towns. But those who are devotees of the Lord, who hunger for spirituality, who burn with the desire and longing to meet the Supreme Being, gather around the saints even at such secluded places. The sandalwood tree may be in a remote corner of the forest, but its fragrance travels far and wide.

Langar

"At whatever place the saints choose to live, they have to start a langar for the sangat, as people who come cannot go without food.

"Babaji Maharaj, seeing that this place was a secluded, barren wilderness, full of deep ravines and gullies, selected it as his

retreat. But those who were seekers of
spirituality began to come to Babaji's feet, even
at this place. Gradually, news about the great
saint and his divine message began to spread,
and seekers started flocking around him. In
order to provide free meals for them, Babaji
opened the langar here, which through his grace
and blessings is still continuing smoothly.

"One of the objects of running the langar
is to provide an opportunity to the satsangis
to serve others. It increases mutual love and
understanding amongst the satsangis. It en-
ables them to rise above the narrow distinctions
of the rich and the poor, of the high and the
low.

Spiritual Centre

"When the Great Master came here, the
satsang flourished even more. Many satsangis
expressed their desire to come and stay at the
Dera. Huzur, therefore, had to build many
houses for the sangat. He also sanctioned the
opening of a small shop to serve milk, butter-
milk, tea and sweets to the sangat. Bhai Arur
Singh, who ran this stall, was a man of saintly
disposition, and was an old devotee and personal attendant of the Great Master. The little
profit he would make from the shop at the end
of the day, he would give in seva. The present
shop of Bhai Mangal Singh is the same shop;
Bhai Arur Singh gave it to him before leaving
this world. Huzur Maharaj Ji did not allow any
other shop to be opened in the Dera.

"Many prominent persons came to the Great Master with industrial projects; some suggested that a school should be opened, others gave suggestions for opening a college. But in response to these suggestions Maharaj Ji always gave the same answer: Babaji Maharaj chose this secluded, quiet place so that the spiritual atmosphere of satsang would always be maintained, and the sangat's attention would not be distracted by other pursuits.

Amenities

"The Great Master's satsang tours were mostly in the regions that are now in Pakistan. After partition of the country, many of his devoted disciples came and settled in cities near the Dera. Therefore, the number of satsangis coming to the Dera suddenly increased, also increasing the needs of the sangat. So, for their convenience and comfort, the Dera organizers made various arrangements.

"You know that to meet your needs we have the Bhojan Bhandar, the tea cafeteria, a general store, a fruit and vegetable market, a provisions store, a cloth shop, and the bookstall. The Dera is trying its utmost to provide everything that you may need while you are here. And so great is Huzur Maharaj Ji's kindness and grace that he gave us a plot of land for the hospital three miles away from the Dera, so that the environment of satsang would not be disturbed in any manner.

Commercial activity discouraged

"But I am much pained to say that seeing the growing number of the sangat, people have begun to open shops in the vicinity of the Dera. This will lead to a harmful development, for gradually these shops will take the shape of a fair. Some will set up shops selling drugs, some liquor, some meat—and all this would lead to undesirable shopping and trading activity on an enormous scale.

"You can go and see the condition of other places of pilgrimage. The people have become oblivious of the real object and purpose for which they visit these holy places. Platforms for state publicity are set up; political parties organize their propaganda booths; wrestling matches are arranged; bazaars for the sale and purchase of cattle are opened.

"My only apprehension is that if these shops outside the Dera continue to grow, some day the spiritual atmosphere of the Dera created by Babaji might disappear.

"That is why responsible Dera sevadars have been repeatedly imploring you not to encourage these shops. And it is both unfortunate and sad that the salesmen at these shops are satsangis, the customers are satsangis, the shop-owners, the suppliers, even the financiers are all satsangis. What then is the difference between us and those places of pilgrimage? If you go there, you will find parshad being sold to the pilgrims for one rupee or five rupees. I have been told that here, in these shops, packets of sweets are being sold as parshad for a rupee a piece.

"If you want to maintain the environment of satsang in the Dera, then all this must be stopped. It is in the hands of the sangat whether it likes to preserve the atmosphere of satsang or wishes to give it the shape of a fair.

"The Dera sevadars and I earnestly desire that the seed of satsang sown by Babaji Maharaj and the pure atmosphere created by him, should continue to thrive. It is now for the satsangis to decide what they wish."

———

Faith in the saints' power of omniscience

There is an interesting incident which happened during the India-Pakistan war of 1971. I was in Bombay when the war began. Maharaj Ji had just had a heart attack and was in hospital at Delhi, in intensive care. Everyone around him was worried and tried to hide the news, thinking that if he came to know of it, he would insist on going to the Dera. But somehow Maharaj Ji came to know and did insist that at such a crucial time, he should be at the Dera. So, in spite of the doctor's advice not to travel, Maharaj Ji took the train from Delhi to Beas.

One of my friends rang me up to say that Maharaj Ji was leaving for Beas, and I immediately became worried as to how I would obtain his permission to go to the Dera once he had reached Beas. Because of the war all forms of communications with the Punjab had been cut off. I was very anxious for darshan, so I rang Maharaj Ji at Mr. Mehta's house, where he was preparing to catch the train, and asked him for permission to come to Beas.

Maharaj Ji said, "You should not come until the war is over."

I replied, "I do not know anything. Please tell me the date on which I should come." That was December the 5th.

Maharaj Ji kept quiet for a second and then said, "Come on the 17th."

Immediately, I rang my office in Bombay and asked them to book me on the Frontier Mail for the 17th.

The manager was much perturbed. He said, "There is a war on and Beas is close to the Pakistan border. How can you think of going? No one is travelling to the Punjab." But on my insistence, he booked my seat.

Accordingly, I informed my husband at Indore, and he joined me at Ratlam on the same train, in spite of his father's objection.

On the 17th, the manager rang me to ask if he should cancel the seat, as the war was still on. I said, "No, Maharaj Ji has allowed me to come on the 17th and come what may, I must leave."

A few satsangi friends also tried to dissuade me from taking the journey. Yahya Khan, the President of Pakistan, was still making statements on the radio that the war would continue until Pakistan won, even if it took six months.

At twelve noon my manager again rang me to ask whether he should cancel the ticket. I said, "I will definitely go. I will not change the date: Maharaj Ji has given me the date on which to come. He also said that I should not come during the war—so I am sure that the war will be before I reach Beas."

In the afternoon (I had not turned on the radio to hear the news) my manager rang me to ask if I had heard the news. He was very excited. I said, "No." Then he told me that the news had just come through on the radio that a cease-fire had been announced. It was in the afternoon, at about 3.00 p.m., and within an hour I had left for the station and reached Beas on the date given by Maharaj Ji. The saints know everything that has to happen, even though they do not always disclose it.

On my arrival at the Dera, I met Mr. R.N. Mehta, who told me all that had happened in Delhi and on their way to Beas. He had accompanied Maharaj Ji from Delhi, along with Maharaj Ji's wife and Dr. Sahani. Maharaj Ji's train reached Beas station at about 9.30 p.m. All the way, after sunset, there had been no lights on in the train. Even the railway stations along the line were all in darkness because of the blackout. At Jullundur, the last stop before Beas, there was pitch darkness all around and they heard the sound of bombardment and anti-aircraft guns. At first, it was announced that the train would not proceed to Beas, but suddenly, after a few minutes, the bombardment ceased and by and by the train moved forward, finally reaching Beas railway station.

Mr. Naidu received Maharaj Ji at the station and made him sit in a wheel-chair to take him to the car, for their drive to the Dera. Later, they were informed that the train had not gone to Amritsar.

Mehta Sahib told me that at the hospital in Delhi, they all had done their best to keep the news of the war from Maharaj Ji. They had even removed the radio from his bedside.

But in the evening one of Maharaj Ji's relatives, Colonel Sidhu, came to call on him, wearing his army uniform. Maharaj Ji asked him, "You retired just a few months ago, how is it that you are in uniform again?"

Mehta Sahib said, "I winked to the Colonel and perhaps he understood, for without replying to this question, he took leave of Maharaj Ji at once, saying that he was in a hurry to go."

Maharaj Ji, however, seemed to have understood, for he at once called the doctor and, getting his suspicions confirmed, told him that he would like to leave for Beas. But the doctor advised him, "As a doctor I cannot let you leave the hospital."

Maharaj Ji argued with him, saying, "You do not understand the whole situation. It is my responsibility to be with the residents of the colony. It is my duty."

Meanwhile, Maharaj Ji's wife also entreated and pleaded with him, saying, "You have suffered such a severe heart attack and are still in intensive care, you should not undertake this strenuous journey. Your health is more important to us than anything else. I realize how anxious you are to be at the Dera, but please listen to the doctor's advice."

Maharaj Ji explained to her, giving a beautiful example. He said, "A soldier is getting married and as the ceremony begins, war is declared and he gets a call to join duty at once. He would not wait for the ceremony of his marriage to be completed, but would immediately leave for his duty. In the same way, to me, my duty is foremost, and I have to be with my people in the Dera at this critical juncture. I must go. Please have no anxiety about me. Leave everything to the Great Master. I have to be at the Dera."

Mehta Sahib took the doctor outside and discussed the details of the situation with him. The doctor advised all of them that there should be no strain of any kind on Maharaj Ji's mind. He said that Maharaj Ji would be more worried about the Dera whilst being here in Delhi than by being there at Beas—and this strain should be avoided at any cost. So it would be better for him to go.

Within half an hour Delhi was plunged in darkness because of blackout. Nevertheless, Maharaj Ji was shifted to Mr. Mehta's house, and the next morning, they all boarded the train to Beas.

The selfless nature of Maharaj Ji impelled him, regardless of thought for his own health, to rush back to the Dera. He knew that his very presence would instill a feeling of security in the hearts of the Dera residents.

――――――

Spirit of sacrifice

Maharaj Ji once said in an English meeting:

"The Great Master laboured hard to spread Sant Mat teachings. He travelled all over the hills of Himachal Pradesh and to various other areas which are now in Pakistan—just on a pony, and sometimes even walking. The roads were very rough.

"I remember once I happened to accompany him to Bahota. There was no fixed satsang schedule. Wherever satsangis collected by the roadside and requested him to hold satsang, he would agree, even though no programme had been arranged.

"It became late and we could not reach Bahota before nightfall. It was getting dark when we came across a group of small huts. There we found twenty or thirty satsangis waiting by the roadside, and they requested the Great Master to stay there for the night. The Great Master agreed to stay there and to hold a satsang.

"Lala Munshi Ram, Bhai Shadi and myself were worried as there was no proper place for the Great Master to stay. Then one of the satsangis came to us

and offered to vacate his house for the Great
Master. He had just one room upstairs, and downstairs was his shop which was filled with merchan-
dise.

"So the upper room was prepared for the Great
Master. And while Lala Munshi Ram and Bhai
Shadi slept downstairs in the shop, I slept under the
Great Master's bed!

"In those days, there were no bathrooms or
latrines in the villagers' houses and people used
to go to the fields for toilet. So we put four poles
in the ground with a white sheet around them.
Then we brought two buckets of water, and with
pieces of stone made a place for the Great Master
to wash.

"Then, in the morning the Great Master got up
as usual, washed, got ready and gave satsang, never
mentioning that he was being put to any inconvenience, while we couldn't sleep all night, thinking,
'How can these people put the Great Master to such
inconvenience?'

"But the Great Master was happy with his
sangat and with their transparent love. The saints are
tied to love—not to places, nor to comfort. This is
how the Great Master spread his teachings to the
remotest corners of distant hills. Now, the seeds that
he has sown are bearing fruit, for thousands and
thousands have become satsangis."

———

Spirit of contentment

On one of Maharaj Ji's visits to Indore, he was accompanied by Mr. Sam Busa, one of his representatives in South Africa. In the evening, Maharaj Ji asked Sam to visit the satsang area and see how things were arranged by the local satsang centre.

It was about ten o'clock at night when Sam, in the company of a sevadar, reached the satsang grounds. Most of the satsangis had retired for the night. Sam was taken around the entire complex and shown all the tents, shamianas and places where the sangat were sleeping. It was a cold February night, and because of the very large gathering of satsangis, enough covered sleeping space was not available. Many satsangis, both young and old, were therefore sleeping under the trees, covering themselves with only a thick cotton sheet.

In the morning, Maharaj Ji asked Sam if he had made a round of the satsang complex. Sam replied, "Yes, Maharaj Ji, I did. But I felt very sad, for people were lying on the bare ground under the tents and even in the open under the trees. It was very cold, and they had only ordinary cotton sheets or mats with which to cover themselves. I was shocked; their standard of living is very poor."

Maharaj Ji smiled softly and said, "Yes, Sam, their standard of living is very poor, but their standard of contentment is very high."

Such simple statements made by Maharaj Ji had deep and meaningful messages, for those who understood them.

Military depot near the Dera

Once, in one of the evening meetings, Maharaj Ji spoke about the current terrorism in the Punjab. He said, "In spite of the whole area around the Dera being infested with terrorists and with so much killing and looting going on every day, by the grace of Babaji Maharaj the Dera has remained an oasis of peace.

"There is a well-protected ammunition depot spread alongside the main road to Beas, and there is always military movement on the road. This keeps the extremists away. Even during the two conflicts with Pakistan, many satsangis came to me and said that due to this military ammunition depot our Dera is always exposed to bombardment. But I replied to them, 'Who knows, it may be due to this that we are safe.' "

This reminds me of some very significant comments made by Sardar Bahadur Ji regarding this depot, and narrated to us by Maharaj Ji. After Babaji died, the Great Master slowly started buying cultivated land from the villages, not only contiguous with the Dera, but wherever he could purchase it. Then, during Sardar Bahadur Ji's time, there was a land consolidation law, whereby farmers' holdings

were to be consolidated all at one place. The Dera
benefited greatly from this, and so the colony sprang
up and spread. But earlier, in 1949, a major portion
of farm land belonging to the Dera had been taken
for this ammunition depot. Additionally, a considerable amount of land belonging to poor farmers
of the neighbouring villages had also been taken
for it.

At that time these farmers approached Lala
Munshi Ram and pleaded, "Please request Sardar
Bahadur Ji to present a petition to free our land. A
lot of Dera land has also been taken."

Lala Munshi Ram approached Sardar Bahadur Ji
and put before him the request of the villagers.
Diwan Daryai Lal Kapoor and Professor Jagmohan
Lal were also there. But Sardar Bahadur Ji said,
"Do not worry, our 'chawkidars' (armed guards)
have come. They will be very useful in the future."

Masters have their own way of anticipating situations much before the need for meeting them arises.
Although they are fully aware and clearly conscious
of the coming events, they sometimes throw veiled
hints which we find difficult to comprehend at that
time.

Maharaj Ji's concern for the sangat

After his heart attack in 1971, Maharaj Ji's
physicians put many restrictions on his satsang
activities.

When Maharaj Ji visited Indore for satsang, Dr. T.N. Mathur accompanied him. Mr. K.L. Khanna, the Dera Secretary at that time, had requested Dr. Mathur to look after Maharaj Ji's health and not to allow him to conduct more than one initiation session per day.

Maharaj Ji had set aside two days for initiation, and his next programme after the Indore satsang was also fixed. But when the initiation started, it was discovered that the number of applicants was larger than expected and could be completed only in four sittings, not in two. When Maharaj Ji came to know of the situation, he said, "I would not like to disappoint the village people who are too poor to bear the expenses of travelling to the Dera." So he decided to give two sittings daily and finish the initiation within the scheduled period of two days.

Dr. Mathur, hearing of Maharaj Ji's decision, protested, saying, "In consideration of your recent heart attack, I earnestly beg of you not to hold two sittings a day."

Maharaj Ji listened patiently and replied in a tone of kindness and love, "Doctor Sahib, when a fisherman throws gram (small roasted chick peas) in the water to attract fish into his net, if the fish gather in large numbers, he does not then refuse to pull in the net, saying that it is too heavy. This he should have realized when he threw the gram into the water. Now he has no option but to haul in the entire load. Now there is no way but to initiate these souls. Do not worry, I will be all right. Doing the Great Master's work never tires me. I am happy to do my duty."

———

The sangat

In response to a question put during an evening meeting, concerning seva and its reward, the Master said, "A lover never asks, a lover never calculates."

In a reminiscent mood, he continued, "I have gone through many experiences. It is more than thirty-five years since I came to the Dera, and the attitude of the sangat, the sangat's love, is something which I cannot describe." Maharaj Ji's voice was filled with love and appreciation.

"In 1955, the langar was very small with only one small gate, yet two lakhs of people would come on the bhandara of the Great Master's birthday. So many would come that they were still feeding them at 2.00 in the morning." Maharaj Ji continued, "I used to be in my bedroom, restless, wondering what should be done to take care of these satsangis who come in the memory of the Great Master.

"This problem was therefore discussed at the annual meeting of the Trust. Mr. Ahluwalia, who was the Secretary at that time, suggested that all the bhandaras should be discontinued to avoid so much rush at one time. 'Let the sangat come at any time they want,' he said. 'This will solve the problem, for then there would be no bhandara rush.' This discussion was going on, and I was just sitting there quietly."

"The news that such a suggestion had been put forward by the Secretary, leaked out to the sangat. The next day, many satsangis crowded around Mr. Ahluwalia at his house. 'Did we ever complain about anything? Have we ever complained about not getting food in time? About not finding a place to sleep? We are happy. Since we have no complaints, why should you propose to discontinue the bhandaras? Why do you want to deprive us of darshan and satsang?'

"The next day Mr. Ahluwalia came to me and said, 'I am sorry for giving that suggestion in the meeting. I withdraw it.'

"I just said, 'I am glad you realized'."

After a short pause, Maharaj Ji continued, "The sangat does not mind any inconvenience. People will sleep on muddy ground, they will sleep in the open under rain, but will never cease coming here. Babaji has laid the foundation of this Dera on love and seva. I have seen this love grow increasingly, ever more and more.

"Look at the 'Mund' (the old river-bed) area. It was full of reeds and tall elephant grass. It was all mud and uneven ground. The sangat used to cut the tall reeds and grass for use as fuel in the langar. Today, the sangat has turned it into level ground, with farms, roads, and tree plantations.

"Where the present langar is today, there were once deep ravines. The sangat has filled and levelled it. The large langar shed and the area where the big trees are growing was all a deep gully. The place where the multipurpose shed has been erected was once a waterway or rill. The sangat has filled it with five or six feet of earth, to make it level. That is seva. You would have to have seen the Dera before, to realize this.

"When the ground for the hospital was acquired, I was told that there were too many trees on the site and that they were very difficult to remove. So I went to the site and I just asked them to remove a few.

"Then I went to Sikanderpur. On my return, I found that about a hundred tractors and trailers had been brought in by the sangat (from their farms), and there were about a thousand satsangis digging up the trees by the roots and loading them onto trailers, taking the wood to the langar. Nobody asked them to do all this. They just came. That is seva.

"The sangat does not do all this seva with the expectation that they will be rewarded. They do it out of love. Seva is love; they never ask for anything in return. And whatever the inconvenience, they never complain. They are always contented, always happy to do the seva."

The power of love, elicited by the Masters and nurtured by the sangat, is without parallel.

A letter from Maharaj Ji to Dr. Schmidt

The following is a copy of an undated handwritten draft of Maharaj Charan Singh's letter to

Dr. Pierre Schmidt, sent shortly after Maharaj Ji's inauguration in November 1951.

"To: Dr. Pierre Schmidt,
       Rue St. Victor 10
       Geneva, Switzerland

"Dear Brother,

"Radha Soami! I thank you most heartily for your very kind letter and for the sentiments and good wishes expressed therein, which I highly appreciate.

"Of course, I will do all that lies in my power to facilitate the spread of Sant Mat truths and bring it within the easy reach of English-knowing and English-speaking people; but I must hasten to tell you, my friend, that I am under no illusions. I have accepted this high office, relying solely on the spiritual help of the Master and the overwhelming love and support of the sangat (congregation).

"Not to talk of that spiritual giant Baba Sawan Singh Ji, our late Master, Sardar Bahadur Baba Jagat Singh Ji possessed a unique person-ality and led such a flawless and austere life that I feel very diffident when I see their mantle falling on my shoulders. His orders came as a surprise to me as I was not present on the spot, and reached here after the cremation was over. In fact, I found no escape and humbly accepted the position, relying on the help and cooperation of friends like you. I made all this absolutely clear in the short speech which I delivered to a crowd of about 60,000 people assembled on the occasion of the Installation Ceremony.

"It makes me very happy to learn that you still think lovingly of the Dera. Need I say that we highly appreciate and reciprocate your sentiments, and hope it shall be possible for you to visit this place again in the near future. I hope your knee is all right by now and you are quite fit, and also able to attend to your bhajan and simran, which is, after all, the only thing that matters.

"It is unfortunate that.....was not able to utilize the privilege of receiving initiation granted by Sardar Bahadur Ji. He wrote here also and was given a suitable reply. There is nothing more to be done in the matter.

"The memory of your last visit is still fresh in my mind, and I look forward eagerly to the possibility of your giving us the pleasure of such a happy meeting again.

"Thanking you for your kindness and sincere cooperation, I remain,

Yours in love and faith"

————

The floods of 1988

During the month of September 1988, there were unprecedented and exceptionally heavy rains in the Punjab and northern India. All the rivers became swollen beyond their capacity, with the result that there were widespread floods. It was all so sudden that everyone was caught unawares. Thousands died, many people were left homeless; property, material and foodstuff were damaged beyond use, and crops were ruined. The Dera, too, was not spared from these floods, though the damage was both minimal and repairable.

Naturally, the Indian newspapers were full of the disaster, and when Maharaj Ji arrived in Delhi for satsang and for his meetings with the foreigners, the question of floods at the Dera was on many people's mind. When one satsangi asked if there had been any flood damage at the Dera, Maharaj Ji replied:

"Well brother, it is very unfortunate—last week we experienced very untimely rains and unprecedented floods. We are still in the middle of this disaster. The Dera was completely cut off by rail and road, by telephone, in every way. There were no telephones for a week or more, the trains are still not running to Beas, and they have just opened the road today. Fortunately, the air service was there and so I am here with you.

"There was so much water in the Beas river that the lower portion of the Dera was under five feet of water. The multi-purpose shed, the ladies shed, and the lower portion of Maharaj Sawan Singh Sarai were all under four to four-and-a-half feet of water. Fortunately, it has receded, but the marks are still there. The whole farm and all the crops were under water. The grain crops had already been harvested, so we did not have to bother about that. There was no damage to any building in the Dera except the lower boundary wall. That has all gone, and we are building a new one. The sevadars are very busy. Actually, I should have been there at this time, but I had to keep this commitment with the sangat and with you people.

"It was very inconvenient for the sangat, because they had all gathered there for the monthly satsang, which was on 25th September. The rains started on 23rd or 24th, and suddenly at 10 o'clock on the night of the 25th the water from the river came two feet deep into the Dera. We had to shift 300 trucks and buses, which were parked outside the Dera, down towards the river. The sevadars worked the whole night, but they salvaged all the buses and trucks which would otherwise have been submerged. We had to shift all the people to the upper portion of the Dera, where fortunately we have a lot of space. We have built a new shed which is practically ready. I had held satsang there on the 25th. So they all shifted there at night.

"Also, we had stored a lot of wheat for our annual consumption. Some of it was in the storerooms situated in the lower portion of the Dera and was spoiled. It fermented and gave an awful smell. That is being dried now, all over

the Dera. It has been spread out on the roads
and is drying in the sun. Let us hope they will
be able to salvage it. Otherwise, they will sell
it for the animals, and we will have to buy new
wheat. But still, with His grace, we have sufficient stock for our langar to continue. There
won't be any shortage of wheat in any way.
So, there was no human loss and we didn't
have any cattle. Our tractors and our farm
machinery were all under water, but they can
be repaired, and that is no problem. In my life
(I am seventy-two now), I have never seen such
floods at the Dera. But by His grace we are all
well. The sangat faced it all very courageously.
They were entrapped from every side, so they
had to stay for about a week in the Dera. Some
of them were very happy that they did not have
to leave the Dera.

"Initiation continued. About 8,000 people
were initiated. And now the roads have been
opened in different directions. The trains have
not yet started again, so practically all the
visitors have moved out of the Dera by road.

"Still, if you read the local papers here,
you will read about an awful picture in
the whole of the Punjab. I can tell you
about the Dera, but other parts of the Punjab
are much worse. It is a horrible sight. The
villages are all surrounded by water. The government is doing its best to alleviate people's
suffering, but the loss is so colossal that I
don't think any government can render that

level of help for the masses. They are trying
to reach people by helicopters. What about
their cattle? What about their food? What
about their clothes and belongings? They
can't be salvaged at all. Many of them have
just been stranded on their rooftops all this
time, without food and shelter. So they are practically washed away, and the danger is always
there of some sort of epidemic such as cholera
or some other disease, spreading after the
floods.

"So we will have to face whatever is in
store for us. Even the district where my farm is,
is quite surrounded by water, but everything is
under control there. Now the water is receding
and the river is quite calm."

***

One evening in October 1988, we were with
Maharaj Ji. Losses due to the floods at the Dera
were on everyone's mind, and Mrs. Bharat Ram
asked Maharaj Ji, "What was the loss to the Dera
because of the floods? It is said to run into millions
of rupees."

Maharaj Ji's reply was typical of his attitude towards human beings as opposed to money. He said:
"Behenji, I only know that there was no loss of
human life in the Dera. That concerns me the most."

In fact, not only was everyone taken care of in
the Dera, but Maharaj Ji also donated ten lakh
rupees to the Punjab Governor's Relief Fund, set up
to help the flood victims. Furthermore, he also sent

truck loads of quilts and clothes to other camps caring for the flood victims.

Human welfare and alleviating the suffering of the people was Maharaj Ji's primary concern, and everything else was secondary. He had great compassion for people undergoing suffering of any kind, whether physical or mental.

Gentle yet firm

It has become customary for people to bring the urns containing the ashes of their dead relatives to the Dera for immersion in the Beas river. When Maharaj Ji is due to come by, they stand at the roadside with the urns in their hands, in the hope of catching a glimpse of him. Whenever Maharaj Ji sees such grief-stricken people, his eyes become filled with tears, though personally he may not know them. He cannot bear to see anyone in anguish.

Maharaj Ji certainly is very soft-hearted, but at the same time he is also a strict disciplinarian. He neither likes, nor tolerates, any kind of indiscipline, in any field of activity. The administration of the Dera is a tremendous example of this. The sangat at bhandara times exceeds three or four lakhs, yet everything in the Dera moves and happens in an orderly fashion. The satsangs are conducted in silence. Hundreds of thousands of people eat in the langar, they live and sleep at the Dera, without any incident or disturbance. The movement of vehicles of all kinds is efficiently and smoothly organized. Despite the multitude, the Dera roads and the whole colony is as clean as it could be, after the bhandara. There is hardly a scrap of paper to be seen anywhere. Of course, there are teams of sevadars managing all the various tasks, but human efforts alone can never achieve such unity of purpose.

Maharaj Ji's presence is the magic and the almost tangible ingredient, which makes everything run like clockwork. His all-pervasive influence, uniting all hearts and minds, is the cohering factor which makes it all hold together. No ordinary human being could engender such a spirit of selfless service and inculcate such love in the hearts and minds of such a multitude. One sees it shining in the eyes and faces of so many people here. Only divinity can inspire such inner unity and love.

All that goes to make the Dera just as Maharaj Ji wants it to be. Life here revolves around him. Therefore, the discipline, cleanliness, beauty, and love are all a reflection of his divine qualities.

Shelter to victims of terrorism — 1987-88

Another example of Maharaj Ji's deep concern for the victims of adverse circumstances is the way he gave shelter at the Dera, in 1987-88, to people who had become terrorists' victims. There were thousands of people in the Punjab whose bread-earning members of the family had been mercilessly killed by terrorists. They were driven out of their homes and deprived of all their belongings.

Maharaj Ji welcomed them at the Dera. At one time, there were about fourteen hundred such people here, uprooted from over a hundred villages. Sikhs, Hindus or Muslims, satsangis or non-satsangis, they were all treated alike. Food, milk, shelter, bedding, medicines and every other possible amenity were provided for the needy. The Dera even opened a temporary school for their children.

The impromptu refugee camp set up at the Dera was one of the best organized in the area. Selfless care, with utter dedication, was carried out by willing sevadars. For quite some time they stayed here until the government took charge of them by instituting a rehabilitation scheme.

This event is again reminiscent of 1947-48, during partition, when the Great Master opened the Dera to all, providing the refugees with food and shelter for as long as they needed. The Great Master also arranged that hot food, prepared at the langar, was sent to the Beas railway station every day, and the sevadars served all transit refugees coming from and going to Pakistan—whether Hindu, Sikh, Muslim, satsangi or non-satsangi. Saints are great humanitarians and they help suffering humanity in every possible way, irrespective of caste or creed.

Maharaj Ji's soft-heartedness is known to all those who have had the privilege of being near or around him. He listens every day to the radio news broadcast which is near about his lunch or dinner time. Many have seen him pushing away his plate on hearing of some calamity or some merciless killing, wherever it might have happened, in any part of the world.

***

One hot and sultry day Maharaj Ji—referring to the weather—commented, "During the summer days I used to slip off to some hill resort, to Dalhousie—the Great Master's kothi is there—or sometimes to my farm at Sirsa. But now I cannot.

"Only last month I had gone to my farm at Sikanderpur for a few days. But the next afternoon there was some terrorist activity in a village near Beas. I received a phone call from the Dera to come immediately. So the next morning I left Sikanderpur and was here before noon.

"Because of the situation in the Punjab, my presence is needed at the Dera, not because of my security, but for the security of the sangat. When I am here, everyone is on his toes, the sevadars are more alert, and the Dera residents feel more secure. Not that I do anything different, but it is my duty to be with the sangat at this time.

"So now I cannot go anywhere. There are armed guards at my gates! They accompany me wherever I go. But I am contented.

"Summer or winter does not make any difference. We should be happy in making others happy, in serving them."

MAHARAJ JI PRACTISING LAW AT SIRSA

Maharaj Ji starts law practice

One day, Maharaj Ji was talking about his college days. He had thought that after graduating in law, but before going to the Bar at Sirsa and settling down, he would travel around India and see a few places. But meanwhile, one of his college friends had been posted to Sirsa as a magistrate, and he suggested to Maharaj Ji's father, "Now that I am here, it would be good for Charan to start his practice right away, as I would also be able to help him."

Maharaj Ji's father agreed that it was a good suggestion and asked Maharaj Ji to settle at Sirsa and—taking whatever furniture, utensils and groceries he needed from the Sikanderpur family home— to make his home in the flat associated with the satsang ghar, which the Great Master had built.

Therefore, Maharaj Ji had no option but to obey his father and forego his plans for travelling.

From the Sikanderpur house, he took whatever he could find, yet lots of things were still needed to furnish the flat. And he also had to buy law books. But he had no money of his own, except a few hundred rupees which he had saved from his pocket money. So he went to Sikanderpur to ask his father for some money, but felt shy and was unable to say anything to him. From childhood he had grown up at the Dera, and the Great Master had looked after all his needs. His school and college fees had all been paid by the Great Master. Actually, it was Bibi Rali who had looked after him and had given him everything, with the permission of the Great Master.

Feeling frustrated, Maharaj Ji came to the Dera. He told Bibi Rali that his father had asked him to stay at Sirsa in the satsang ghar flat and to practise law, but he had not given him any money. "And there are lots of things I need to buy," he told her. "Crockery, curtain cloth and so on—and I have to buy books, too. What should I do? I went to Sikanderpur, but felt shy to ask Chachaji (as Maharaj Ji called his father) because never in my life have I asked him for anything. So I have come here."

Bibi Rali went to the Great Master and told him everything Maharaj Ji had said. The Great Master laughed and replied: "A son who could not ask his father for money! Call him here."

Maharaj Ji came and the Great Master asked him, "How much money do you want?"

Maharaj Ji replied, "About four thousand rupees." So the Great Master gave this amount to him.

Maharaj Ji then returned to Sirsa, bought whatever was needed and settled in. After a few days, his father visited him and asked him why he had gone to the Dera so soon after his previous visit only a fortnight before. Maharaj Ji said, "I needed some money."

His father asked, "Why did you not ask me when you came to Sikanderpur?"

Maharaj Ji replied, "I had come to ask you, but did not know how to ask, because I have never asked you for anything in my entire life."

Then Maharaj Ji's father told him, "In future, please take whatever you need—do not hesitate."

Today, Maharaj Ji's nature still remains the same. For himself, he would still hesitate to ask for anything, even from his own family account.

Maharaj Ji's illness

Maharaj Ji once told us that in June 1946, when he was practising as a lawyer, he had gone to Hissar district court to attend a case. Being summer, the weather was extremely hot—especially in that part of India. When he came out of the courtroom, he started to discuss some point with another lawyer, when suddenly he fainted, and fell down. One of the lawyers, who hardly knew him, took him to his house where he and his wife looked after him with much care and affection. He was running a very high temperature, and they did whatever they possibly could, keeping him in their house for four days.

They wrote a letter to Maharaj Ji's wife, telling her of his condition and requesting her to come. Then Maharaj Ji's father came to see him, and when he was feeling a little better, his cousin Satnam Singh came and took him to Sirsa, where he suddenly developed smallpox. It spread all over his body and his whole face was covered, even his eyes, and of course he was still running a high temperature.

When Maharaj Ji's mother came to know, she asked his wife to shift him to Sikanderpur, so that she could look after him and give him home treatment, as she did not have much faith in the usual medicines. Hence, Maharaj Ji was brought to Sikanderpur, where he was kept in a dark room, as advised by Dr. Mathur and Maharaj Ji's mother. At that time, Dr. Mathur was stationed at Sirsa and he often came by bicycle to see Maharaj Ji, the distance between Sirsa and Sikanderpur being about five miles. Maharaj Ji was worried that his whole face would be pock-marked and that he might even lose his eyesight. He said that he did not dare to look into the mirror.

He asked his wife to write a letter to Bibi Rali, describing his condition—how his face was disfigured by smallpox, how worried he was about it, how he would live with a pock-marked face, what he would do in life, and how it may even affect his eyesight. He also requested her to seek the Great Master's permission to come and look after him because he missed her.

Bibi Rali took the letter to the Great Master and read it. The Great Master said, "He is a grown-up man, yet he is still so attached to you? Write to him that he will be all right within ten days, that there will be no marks left on his body, and that he should come here after ten days."

Professor Jagmohan Lal was also with the Great Master when Bibi Rali read Maharaj Ji's letter to him. Professor Sahib was very fond of Maharaj Ji, so he also wrote to him, telling him not to worry as

the Great Master had said he would be absolutely all right.

Maharaj Ji said that the letter arrived, and after ten days the fever had subsided and all the marks of smallpox had disappeared with the exception of one on his little toe. Thereafter, Maharaj Ji came to Beas to see the Great Master.

The Great Master said, "It will be all right in the morning. You get perturbed very easily."

Maharaj Ji told us, "By the morning the mark had disappeared. It was indeed a miracle that in spite of my body and face being fully covered with deep pock-marks, I do not even have one mark left on my body."

_____

Hesitation to accept successorship

When we hear a Master's spontaneous refusal or disinclination to take up his position, even though instructed to do so by his Master, we may find it difficult to understand that here we are seeing true humility in action. But it is their genuine reaction and it is also a great lesson for us.

After Sardar Bahadur Ji's will had been read and Maharaj Ji had come to know for certain that he had been nominated as the next Master, he refused pointblank to accept the 'gaddi'. He wept bitterly and was so adamant about it that he even ran away from the Dera. Maharaj Ji's reaction has been recounted earlier.

Seeing his state of mind, his father and mother requested Rai Sahib Munshi Ram to permit them to take Maharaj Ji to Sikanderpur for a few days. This was on the third day after the cremation of Sardar Bahadur Ji. In her heart, his mother felt disturbed to see him in this condition. Mrs. Hazara Singh, who treated Maharaj Ji like her own son, also came from Ambala to join the family at Sikanderpur.

After reaching the farm, Maharaj Ji's father tried to reason gently with him, asking, "After receiving initiation from the Great Master, does this body belong to the Great Master or to ourselves?" Maharaj Ji replied, "To the Great Master."

So, with tears in his eyes, his father said, "In that case, what objection can you have to carrying out whatever work the Great Master wishes to take from this body?"

Maharaj Ji kept quiet as there was nothing he could add. Then his father bowed his head before him and left the room. Similarly, the whole family gave him their support; his wife also persuaded him to accept the position, assuring him that she would cooperate in every way.

After Maharaj Ji's inauguration, his father told him not to worry about the welfare of his children and his wife, saying that his brother Shoti would take good care of them. Maharaj Ji says that, to his great credit, he has done this very well.

Maharaj Ji and his entire family wholeheartedly aligned themselves to the will of the Great Master,

GREAT MASTER WITH MAHARAJ JI'S FATHER, MAHARAJ JI AND RAO SAHIB

and to this day Maharaj Ji spends his every waking minute serving the sangat as instructed by the Great Master, lovingly performing all his duties in order to please his Master.

Sheltering the Sikanderpur Muslims

At the time of partition, in 1947, there was great turbulence and unrest throughout India, arising out of conflict between the Hindu and Muslim communities. Age-old prejudices, unreasoning hatreds and jealousies erupted into rioting and violence, the killing of people and the destruction of property on an unprecedented scale. Nobody felt safe.

At that time, the major part of the population of Sikanderpur and about a dozen nearby villages was Muslim. There were only one or two Hindu families, and Maharaj Ji's family was the only Sikh household in the area. They were only about twenty-five in number including the ladies.

One day, the village panchayat (village elders) from Sikanderpur came to Maharaj Ji's father, seeking shelter for their Muslim community, and requesting him to look after their belongings, their property and their land. All around them, Muslims, Hindus and Sikhs were engaged in one of the bloodiest massacres in Indian history. For Muslims to make such a request to a Sikh family was truly remarkable, and speaks volumes for the regard in which the Great Master's family was held.

Maharaj Ji, at that time, was living at Sirsa, about five miles from the Sikanderpur farm, where he was practising law. The Deputy Commissioner (D.C.) and the Superintendant of Police (S.P.) were both amongst Maharaj Ji's friends. So his father sent him a message, asking him to arrange police protection for these Muslims as well as for his own family, in case any of the local Muslims should start any trouble.

Maharaj Ji, therefore, approached the D.C. and the S.P. with his father's request. But because of the unrest all around, they had no men to spare, and could only suggest to him that he may take a police truck to Sikanderpur, collect all his family members and return with them to Sirsa.

Maharaj Ji knew that his father would never accept such a proposal. When he told him, he rejected it, being adamant that he would not leave their home. He also added that he had sent a man with a letter to the Great Master asking him what he should do, and was expecting a reply the next day.

The Great Master's response arrived as expected. He wrote that Maharaj Ji's father should look after all the Muslims in the village. No harm should come to them from anyone. They are all under his protection. He also asked Maharaj Ji's father to tell everyone at the farm that no harm of any sort would befall any of them. He wrote, "Nobody will even touch a hair. Do not worry, Babaji is with you." This assurance, of course, was a source of great comfort and solace to them.

So Maharaj Ji's father comforted everyone, saying, "Please do not worry about anything. No one will harm you or do anything untoward to you." He then asked his men to take turns to keep watch on the village at all times, and to see that no outsiders could come and create any kind of trouble.

He also opened his flour-grinding mill for the use of these Muslim villagers, since they had no way of making wheat flour for their bread, and provided whatever other help was needed, while they were there. In addition, he told Maharaj Ji to ask the D.C. and the S.P. at Sirsa to give them a safe escort to join a caravan, whenever one was passing on its way to Pakistan.

But as events turned out, Maharaj Ji and Chacha Amar Singh themselves escorted these Muslims when word came that the Baloch Muslim regiment was passing by on the main road on their way to Pakistan, and handed over the villagers to their care. They all had tears of gratitude in their eyes, and were extremely grateful to Maharaj Ji's father for taking such good care of them and for seeing them safely on the road to Pakistan.

There were a few old men and women, unable to undertake the journey, so they were left behind by the villagers in the care of Maharaj Ji's father. Maharaj Ji's mother looked after them throughout their life, providing them with whatever they needed. In fact, many Muslim satsangi families did not go to Pakistan at all, and Maharaj Ji says that they are still living happily in the village of Sikanderpur.

For saints, it is only human lives which matter. They are not concerned with caste or creed, with rich or poor. To them, all people are the same and they are always ready to help everyone. By their example, they teach us the same lesson. Maharaj Ji's father was a true disciple of the Great Master and followed his example perfectly, inspiring his family to do the same.

———

The perfect disciple

One day, in a reminiscent mood, Maharaj Ji said that during his childhood he had developed the impression that his father did not love him; and this feeling lingered in his mind for quite a few years.

Maharaj Ji and his brother grew up together at the Dera, under the loving care of the Great Master. Both the brothers were sent to school together at Balsarai, a distance of about a mile from the Dera, which they used to walk. They joined school at Baba Bakala in the fifth class.

On reaching the sixth class, Maharaj Ji's brother was moved to Jullundur for further studies, while Maharaj Ji stayed on at the same school until he reached the tenth class. Naturally, as a child, Maharaj Ji felt this difference in treatment between himself and his brother, because Baba Bakala was only a very small village, while Jullundur was a city.

His brother was even given a bicycle, while Maharaj Ji still had to walk to school. During all this time, his father never made any inquiry about his studies or showed any fatherly interest in his activities. Maharaj Ji could not understand this disinterested behaviour on the part of his father, and it used to hurt him.

Then, when proposals for Maharaj Ji's engagement began to arrive, his father again showed no interest. Finally, when the Great Master arranged his engagement to Rao Sahib's daughter, Harjeet Kaur, his mother and father were not at the Dera, and the Great Master had not even consulted them.

Similarly, on the previous evening, the Great Master had arranged the engagement of Maharaj Ji's younger sister, Gurnam Kaur, without consulting their parents.

After his engagement when Maharaj Ji went to Sirsa and told his father that he and Gurnam were both engaged, his father just accepted it without asking anything about the family into which he had been engaged or concerning any other details. Nor did he show the pleasure which a father would normally feel.

Maharaj Ji was naturally disconcerted about his attitude, feeling that his father had no interest in him. Even when Maharaj Ji was practising as a lawyer at Sirsa, his father never asked him how he was faring in his practice or how much he was earning.

It was only when Maharaj Ji was asked by the

Great Master to leave his legal practice and help his father in running the farm, and he came to live at Sikanderpur with his father, that he began to realize that his father not only had no interest in him, but also had no interest in anybody at all—neither in his family members, nor in family matters. Indeed, he gave his entire annual income to the Great Master, not keeping anything for himself.

His sole interest and focus of devotion was the Great Master, who was also his father. He was a unique example of a perfect disciple. His total surrender to his Satguru and his obedience were perfect. His whole life and interest revolved around the Great Master. His only attachment was to the Great Master and not to anyone or anything else at all. He never took any interest in anything unless it had some connection or association with the Great Master. Such was his single-minded devotion.

Maharaj Ji added, "If I ever asked him anything, the usual answer was, 'Ask the Great Master and act accordingly.' "

Maharaj Ji went on to say that his father accepted the Great Master's will in total surrender, though he possessed a strong mind. He did not shed a tear at the passing away of his eldest son-in-law. He just accepted it as his Master's will. But when the Great Master passed away, he wept bitterly and his grief was inconsolable. He lost all interest in living, and during Sardar Bahadur Ji's time he started practically to live at the Dera.

Seeing his father in a new light, Maharaj Ji developed a high regard for him, as he understood that his father's only love was the Great Master, and that nothing else mattered to him.

He suffered from diabetes and whenever Maharaj Ji suggested consulting doctors and taking better medical advice, he would always reply, "What is the use of living without the Great Master?" and would not agree to consult them.

Maharaj Ji further added that after he had come to the Dera as the Master, his father never looked upon him as a son. He always gave Maharaj Ji the same respect which he had given to the Great Master, loving him in the same way. There could be no better example of a true disciple and, Maharaj Ji added, even of a father, to accept his son as his Master—as the Lord Himself.

During his last days, Maharaj Ji said that he had asked his father whether he would like to give him any advice, or if he had any last wish. He replied to Maharaj Ji, "I would like you and your brother always to live together with love and affection. Even if Shoti is unreasonable sometimes, forgive him. You are his elder brother and should overlook his shortcomings, if any."

Maharaj Ji said that by the grace of the Great Master, there has always been understanding and love between them. There has never been any misunderstanding.

A unique disciple was Maharaj Ji's father. Such devotion is entirely the result of the Master's grace and is not commonly to be found in this world.

Excerpts of letters to Maharaj Ji
from his father

Translated from Urdu, the following are extracts from handwritten letters to Maharaj Ji from his father, soon after he had become the Master. What father writes to his son in such a way? Only one with perfect devotion, accepting him unreservedly as the Lord Himself, could address his son like this.

June 14th, 1952

"Bowing my head on the all-powerful lotus feet of kind and merciful Satguru Ji, I humbly offer a million Radha Soamis with folded hands.

"By the grace of ever kind and merciful Huzur, I am well. Your benign letter has been received; I was immensely happy to read it. . . .

"This slave greatly feels that he could not present himself in your august presence and service. It was purely my weakness and the·shackles of worldly responsibilities. . . . I hope you will have mercy and forgive my shortcomings.

Your servant"

September 20th, 1953 (a postcard)

"I place my head on the lotus feet of revered Satguru Ji and humbly submit my Radha Soami. . . .

Your slave"

September 25th, 1953

"Revered Huzur Maharaj Tikka Sahib Ji,
Radha Soami with folded hands. Trust you must
have reached there comfortably and safely. . . .
Huzur's work here is progressing satisfactorily. . . .
When will I get your darshan? You had told me
that you would be coming to Sikanderpur every
second or third month. So it should be, at least
while I live. But you are the Lord; I am just a
watchman in your household. . . .

Your servant"

June 2nd, 1955

"Revered Huzur Maharaj Tikka Sahib Ji,
Radha Soami with folded hands. Trust that you are
keeping well. It is your kindness and grace that you
have remembered me. . . .

Your obedient servant"

———

Maharaj Ji's great love for his Master

In one of the evening meetings with the foreigners, a satsangi asked Maharaj Ji a question
concerning the Dera administration after the passing
away of the Great Master. Maharaj Ji replied that
the vacuum was so great—and then he broke down.
His voice was choked and he could not speak. With
his hand he gestured to the satsangi not to persist in

his questioning, and in a voice filled with emotion he asked Professor Bhatnagar to read and translate from one of the saints.

Later, the satsangi expressed his reaction to Maharaj Ji's response in a letter. It is worth sharing, and with Maharaj Ji's permission this is reproduced below:

> "I am the person who asked you the question the other evening concerning life at the Dera during the days of Maharaj Jagat Singh. Firstly, I am very sorry if my question was inappropriate and/or caused you any pain or embarrassment. I know that none of us will ever forget that evening. It was beautiful for us to see your love for your Master.

> "In my life, I feel a need to learn to feel and cry more and I hope that to be a lesson to me. I also hope to love my Master with just a fraction of the love that you have for yours.

> "My question is, 'How can I open my heart to feel more love?' I very much appreciate all that you give to me."

Masters' concern for their disciples

Masters always look after the welfare of their disciples as if they were their own children. They are always there to help them in difficulties, often without the disciple being aware of it. To thousands of those families uprooted from what is now Pakistan, such help was given by the Great Master, in one way or another, in getting them settled in other parts of India.

One such example is that of the Mehta family, who were—and still are—deeply devoted initiates of the Great Master. The Mehtas originally came from Rawalpindi, now in Pakistan, and from Kashmir. In the partition of India, Kashmir has always been a hotly debated territory. Indeed, it is still subject to continuous border disputes and, at the time of partition, raiders came from Pakistan to attack the inhabitants of Kashmir. This was anticipated, and they had just reached the border with India when the entire Mehta family, with their wives and children, escaped by night in three fully loaded cars, numbering about twenty-four persons in all. They were carrying hardly anything with them. Driving through the night, they came directly to the Amritsar Satsang Ghar, where they knew that the Great Master was staying. Maharaj Ji was there with him.

Upon their arrival, the Great Master called Maharaj Ji and said to him, "Your friends have come. Take them to Sikanderpur and take care of their families, so that the men can go to Delhi and look for some business."

So Maharaj Ji took them all to Sikanderpur and the families of all the Mehta brothers stayed there for several months, while R.N. Mehta and R.C. Mehta went to Delhi to find a shop where they could start a photography business, as they had been well-known photographers in Kashmir and Rawalpindi.

Incidentally, back in 1945 the Government had stopped the circulation of 1000 rupee notes in an attempt to check the circulation of black money. R. N. Mehta had therefore sent R. C. Mehta, accompanied by Mataji (their elder sister), with 80,000 rupees in 1000 rupee notes to be handed over to Maharaj Ji, asking him to keep the money, but without giving him any explanation.

Maharaj Ji put the money in his father's account without telling him anything. And it was this money which helped the Mehta family to set up their business, as well as themselves and their families, in Delhi.

Maharaj Ji also added that they had completely trusted him with all that money. They had left it without asking for a receipt of any kind. Today, everyone knows how well the Mehta family is settled, and how they have become such dedicated and loving sevadars of the Master.

The importance of birthdays

After their death, the birthdays of some Masters become occasions for celebration, often by killing living beings for eating and by excessive drinking. Maharaj Ji is fond of pointing out, with considerable humour, that Christmas day is celebrated by the slaughter of thousands of turkeys, by eating and drinking to excess, and by intense commercial exploitation.

Maharaj Ji has never given any importance to his birthday. In fact, he has characteristically done his best to be absent from the Dera on his birthday so that nobody should make a fuss.

Once, when Maharaj Ji was planning a satsang tour abroad, he gave his passport to Mrs. Bharat Ram, so that she could arrange for the necessary visas. Out of curiosity, I picked it up and on looking through it, was amazed to see that his date of birth was given as August 16th, 1916, for, as is well known, his date of birth is actually December 12, 1916. So I asked him why the date on his passport was different.

He replied that when he had passed the matriculation examination and had been given the requisite certificate, he brought it to the Great Master. The Great Master expressed his pleasure, because Maharaj Ji was the first boy in the family to pass his matriculation exam. But when the Great Master looked closely at the certificate, he asked Maharaj Ji, "How is it that both your name and date of birth are written incorrectly? Your name is Harcharan Singh, while here it is written as Charan Singh. And your date of birth is December 12th, 1916, while here it is given as August 16th, 1916."

Maharaj Ji knew nothing about it, so the Great Master made inquiries and discovered how the confusion had arisen. Bhai Shadi, who was a personal attendant of the Great Master, had been sent with Maharaj Ji on his first day at Balsarai School, to arrange for his formal admission. But he himself was quite illiterate. When the Great Master questioned him, he replied simply that the teacher had asked Maharaj Ji's name. He had told the teacher that he was called 'Charani', which was Maharaj Ji's pet name. So the teacher assumed that his name was Charan Singh and wrote it down accordingly.

Then the teacher asked for the boy's date of birth. Bhai Shadi replied, "Write today's date"— which happened to be August 16th. This mistake remained unnoticed throughout his school days, even into high school, and was reproduced faithfully on his matriculation certificate!

The Great Master wanted the record to be put straight. So he called Sardar Bhagat Singh, as the Great Master always consulted him on the legal aspects of the Dera and family matters. He had great confidence in him. So he asked him to have the name and date of birth corrected.

Sardar Bhagat Singh made inquiries and discovered that once a university enrollment number had been issued to a student on a matriculation certificate, it became a very complicated procedure to have any of the particulars regarding his name and date of birth changed. He therefore advised that the matter be left as it was.

Thus, Maharaj Ji's official name and date of birth continued to be as they were recorded on his matriculation certificate.

Maharaj Ji's uncomplaining nature

Maharaj Ji once related that he had had to go to school on foot. Several times Bhuaji (Bibi Rali) suggested to the Great Master that he should buy a bicycle for him, but every time the proposal was turned down with the reply, "I want him to become hardy," even though Maharaj Ji's younger brother, who was studying at Jullundur, already had a bicycle.

When Maharaj Ji had reached the ninth class, Bibi Rali told the Great Master that the Dera carpenter's son and the blacksmith's son—who were Maharaj Ji's class fellows—both had bicycles to go to school. Then the Great Master agreed to get a bicycle for Maharaj Ji as well. But until then, he had walked the three miles to school every day, which goes to show how obedient and uncomplaining Maharaj Ji was, even as a child.

Gratitude to the Lord even in adversity

Maharaj Ji always says that we should be grateful to the Lord for whatever He gives us. At every step in our lives we should feel gratitude; whether the turn of events appears to us to be good or bad should be no concern of ours. We do not know the spiritual good which may be hidden behind the apparently bad—and vice versa. So we should make our best efforts to live in His will, and be thankful to Him for whatever He has arranged in our destiny. In this respect, Maharaj Ji narrated an incident from the life of the great Moghul Emperor, Shah Jahan.

Shah Jahan ruled over a vast empire in India, reaching far into the south. He was a great builder and some of the most beautiful architectural marvels in the medieval period were built by him. Probably the most famous of all are the Taj Mahal at Agra and the Red Fort at Delhi.

After ruling for several decades, his son Aurangzeb could no longer control his desire to be the Emperor and usurped the throne by force, imprisoning his father in the fort at Agra.

Shah Jahan passed the remainder of his days as a prisoner, devoid of all royal comforts, being forced to lead a very spartan life. He no longer lived in the splendour of the court, nor had a retinue of courtiers and servants to attend on him.

One hot summer afternoon, Shah Jahan was feeling very thirsty, but there was no one available to give him water. So he himself went to the well in the prison and started drawing water. But the ex-emperor, unaccustomed to the simple skills of drawing water, let slip the rope from the wheel. The bucket, out of control, swung towards him, delivering a resounding crack to his head.

At this, Shah Jahan exclaimed, "Oh Lord! I am not even good for simple things like drawing water from the well, yet you made me an Emperor for such a long time. I offer a million thanks to

you for your grace and mercy to me." Saying this,
Shah Jahan bowed his head in obeisance to the
Lord.

The marked sheep

Maharaj Ji was once travelling by train to
Dehra Dun on his way to Mussoorie. While travelling he became acquainted with an affectionate
lady—Mrs. Hazara Singh. The acquaintance developed over the course of time into one of great
affection. Maharaj Ji became very fond of her, and
she loved him as her own son.

Maharaj Ji called her Biji, a term also used for
'mother' in the Punjab. She visited Maharaj Ji
several times at the Dera, and he also used to visit
her home. Mrs. Hazara Singh was a lady of deep
religious sentiment and regularly read the Japji
Sahib, from the Adi Granth. She met the Great
Master on several occasions, developing great love
and respect for him.

Maharaj Ji was keen to stand in the elections of
1945, but had to relinquish the idea because of
an unexpected Government ordinance. Naturally,
he was disappointed and not in a cheerful mood.
On hearing of this, Biji—concerned about his dis-
composure—travelled to Sirsa to spend some time
with him.

The Great Master at that time was on tour and
on his way to Peshawar (now in Pakistan). Learning
of Maharaj Ji's disappointment, he sent a message to

him, asking Maharaj Ji to join him on his tour. So Maharaj Ji went to Peshawar and Biji, too, went along with him.

Because of his affection for her, Maharaj Ji entertained a keen desire that the Great Master should give her Nam. So Maharaj Ji told Bhai Shadi of his wish as to how wonderful it would be if the Great Master would give her Nam.

That evening, Maharaj Ji and Bhai Shadi were pressing the Great Master's legs, as was their usual practice. The Great Master was in an informal mood, so Shadi took advantage of the opportunity and told him of Maharaj Ji's wish. But the Great Master replied, "Tell him, he may initiate her himself."

Maharaj Ji was greatly surprised to hear such a response from the Great Master and could not understand its meaning. Then, after a while, the Great Master continued, telling him that it was not in her destiny to receive Nam in this life.

When Maharaj Ji came to the Dera, after the passing away of Sardar Bahadur Ji, Biji was a regular visitor, remaining here for long periods of time. On several occasions she mentioned to Maharaj Ji that she would like to receive Nam, but for one reason or another the opportunity did not arise, and she passed away without being initiated.

To be initiated by a perfect Master signals the end of our coming and going in the cycle of birth and death. It is the most significant event in the

history of a soul since it left the Lord at the time
of creation. The moment of initiation is destined,
and the Masters know exactly when that moment
will come.

————

Sant Mat avoids politics

In their great wisdom, the Masters have always
kept themselves aloof from politics. Their interest is
in the relationship of the individual soul with the
Lord, not in the divisive political interests of individuals or groups in this world. Maharaj Ji, too, has
handled all his association with political leaders with
great care, circumspection and discernment.

From time to time, political leaders have come
to the Dera to meet Maharaj Ji, especially at
election times, seeking his blessings and, more
particularly, his support. But Maharaj Ji has never
involved either himself or the satsang in politics,
always maintaining the highest degree of spiritual
integrity and the purity of Sant Mat teachings. Under
his sagacious guidance and protection, the affairs of
satsang have always remained aloof from politics.

Before he came to the Dera as Satguru, Maharaj
Ji had been persuaded by members of a prominent
political party to stand for election. In fact, there
was a fair chance of his being elected as a member
of the provincial assembly, but Sardar Bahadur Ji
had strongly rejected the suggestion.

On hearing that Maharaj Ji had become the new

spiritual head of the Dera, the same politicians who had earlier wanted Maharaj Ji to stand in the elections came to the Dera. They told Maharaj Ji how happy they we're that he was the new head of the Dera. They then requested him that as the leader of such a large number of people, he should instruct them all to vote 'en bloc' for the party candidate.

Maharaj Ji replied to the delegation that he was unable to give any such directions to the sangat, as his relationship with the satsangis was entirely, and only, spiritual. The individual satsangi's alignment or otherwise to any particular political party and how he casts his vote, or whether he altogether abstains, is entirely his personal affair. He pointed out that he could not interfere with an individual's freedom and prerogative to cast his vote in any way he considered fit.

The politicians were dismayed and almost insisted that Maharaj Ji make an appeal to the sangat. No doubt they thought, as is the worldly practice, that having once supported Maharaj Ji, he should now repay the debt of gratitude.

Maharaj Ji, with his usual sagacity and legal acumen, pointed out that bringing any religious influence or pressure to bear upon any community of voters would, according to the constitution of India, make such an election void. The leaders then realized Maharaj Ji's point of view and the force of his argument.

Since then, Maharaj Ji has made this point of view absolutely clear to the sangat many times. He himself has announced in satsangs that the votes of citizens are their personal right, which they should exercise as they wish. The announcements are circulated to all the satsang centres in India.

For instance, with the approach of the Indian General Election of November 1989, Maharaj Ji made the following announcement to the enormous gathering, numbering in the region of 300,000, who had assembled at the Dera for the bhandara held on October 29th, 1989:

"Before starting the satsang I want to make a very important submission. Please listen carefully to what I say. Before every election in the past I have reminded the sangat that Radha Soami Satsang Beas has no connection whatsoever with politics and has always kept itself aloof from elections. All political parties are ours. I have the same regard and affection for all of them. But my relationship with the sangat, with the satsang, is that of spirituality, of love and devotion. It is not a relationship of votes. Your vote is your personal prerogative. You are free to give it to anyone you like.

"Please keep politics out of satsang. No satsangi brother should try to bring any politician to me. My effort has always been to keep the satsang free from political involvement, and with the grace and blessings of the Great Master, the satsang has remained aloof from politics. And I am anxious to maintain that aloofness. Therefore, you may give your vote to

160TREASURE BEYOND MEASUREany candidate of your choice, but please do not try to involve the satsang with politics."

Senior staff members admonished

Some prominent Dera sevadars, in spite of all their efficiency and alertness, are occasionally observed to lose their temper, forgetting the high ideals of seva, and behaving haughtily with the sangat.

Maharaj Ji had been receiving letters of complaint from satsangis and therefore, on September 26th, 1987, he made the following remarks during satsang:

"Often, old satsangis come and tell me, 'You lay so much stress on humility and seva, so why do you not/teach it to your staff members? They do not even greet each other with a loving Radha Soami, not to say of listening to our problems.'

"When I hear such things, I also wonder what the matter is. All the members of the Dera staff are good, hard-working people and they have great love for the Dera. In their working life, they have held senior and responsible positions and have come here after retirement.

"Then it occurred to me that in the times of the Great Master and Sardar Bahadur Ji, the office-cum-residence consisted of only two small rooms—one in the back and another at the front. In the back room, Rai Sahib Har Narayan used to live, and after him, Rai Sahib Munshi Ram. Their office consisted of one room only. For their work, they had just a small wooden platform on the verandah. And for fifty or sixty years they carried on their work while sitting on that dais, which was covered only by a thin cotton mattress.

"Now I have built an elegant secretariat. All officers have their own independent rooms with marble flooring. They are provided with all facilities. And they have been given chairs of authority.

"But from their earlier positions of authority during their working days, they have come straight to the Dera and occupied their chairs here. Perhaps it is entirely my fault that I did not give them an opportunity to learn what seva at the Dera really means and what seva actually is. Seva consists of humility, of dedication."

Hearing Maharaj Ji's words in the satsang, the faces of the prominent sevadars fell and Maharaj Ji, sensing their suddenly changed serious mood, narrated the following anecdote:

"Three or four months ago, a satsangi from Doaba came to me and told me something amusing, which made me laugh. He said, 'I am very sad because my father has passed away.' He then added, 'My relatives gave in charity neither bedding, nor a pair of shoes, nor even any cooking utensils.'

"To begin with, I could not understand what he was saying. But when I thought it over, I realized that he was referring to a local superstition regarding the needs of a departed person.[1]

"So, out of sympathy, I said, 'The poor departed man, without bedding—where must he be sleeping? Without cooking utensils, how must he be preparing his food? Without shoes, he must be walking barefoot.'

"The satsangi then told me that his dead father was a disciple of the Great Master and so perhaps he had provided his father with all these things.

"I replied, 'If the Great Master has taken care of him, would he not give him bedding? Would he not give him a pair of shoes or provide him with cooking utensils? But in what delusions have you entangled yourself? Even after coming here, you have not been able to rid yourself of these superstitions and false beliefs.' "

On hearing this tale, the sangat and sevadars all roared with laughter at the man's folly and everyone went away with a light heart.

The next day, Mrs. Bharat Ram asked Maharaj Ji, when we were sitting in his verandah, "Maharaj Ji, you are always appreciative of the services of

---

1. In India, the priestly class exploit the superstitious nature of simple people by telling them that the departed soul will lack bedding, cooking utensils and so on, unless they give these things in charity to the priests.

your staff members, then how is it that you dealt with them so harshly in satsang?"

Maharaj Ji replied, "Behenji, individually all the members of my staff are pure gold. They are hard-working, honest and loyal to the institution. My feeling is only this: When I bring them together, they do not cooperate with one another. Sometimes they differ violently with each other even in my presence.

"I have been trying for a long time to get all the members of my staff to feel a joint responsibility in the administration of their departments. But some of them are so conscious of their authority and so sensitive to any suggestion given to them that they even defy the instructions of the secretary.

"Sometimes I feel that perhaps it is my fault that immediately upon their retirement, I elevated them to high positions in the Dera administration, without giving them any opportunity to grow up from the grass roots, in their seva.

"I think that gradually they will improve. Even otherwise, I am going to change the entire pattern of Dera administration, by making all the heads of departments independent. If any problems arise, they can seek guidance either from the secretary or from me."

Rituals and ceremonies

Maharaj Ji spoke in the satsang this morning concerning our human tendency to give importance to rituals and external religious practices, thus ignoring the real teachings of spirituality given by the saints. The outward tendency of the mind is so ingrained that it readily develops external habits and conventions which—in the absence of inner spiritual practice—soon become rituals and ceremonies. These, the mind comes to feel, are the only right and proper ways of worship.

Maharaj Ji commented in the satsang that Babaji had made it very clear to his sevadars that they were not to erect any memorial at the place of his cremation. During his lifetime, Babaji had observed that people—in the absence of a perfect Master to guide them—had started building a 'samadhi' or mausoleum at the place of Soami Ji's cremation. These people were thus drifting away from the teachings of Soami Ji.

The Dera cremations have always been performed in the old river bed, and Maharaj Ji said that after the cremation of Babaji, when people went the next day to collect the ashes, they found that during the night the river had completely run over the spot, removing any trace of the ashes. Nobody could find the place of his cremation.

Even in some satsang centres, a tendency develops towards the performance of external formalities and a ceremonial way of doing things. In the absence of clear, simple and perceptive thinking, the natural desire to show respect and honour to the Master is easily channelled through the external, ritualized behaviour to which individuals are inclined.

Seeing this, Maharaj Ji said that the Great Master had received a firm promise from Rai Sahib Munshi Ram that no memorial or samadhi would be erected in his memory. "Many disciples of the Great Master are present today," added Maharaj Ji, "who will recall that on the eighth or ninth day after his cremation, there was a tremendous dust-storm and gale. After the storm had subsided, the bamboo poles and buntings which had been placed at the site were nowhere to be seen. The features of the area had also changed so much that the actual place of his cremation could not be located.

"Some people said that it was at one place, others claimed that it was at another. Today, nobody can tell whether the river consumed that spot or it has been incorporated into the agricultural farmland.

"Similarly," Maharaj Ji went on to say, "Sardar Bahadur Ji dictated specific instructions to Rai Sahib Munshi Ram, shortly before he left his body. It is the custom in India to wash the body of one who has just died and dress it in clean clothes, in preparing it for cremation. To avoid this ceremony, Sardar Bahadur Ji took a bath, shortly prior to his passing away, and put on clean clothes. Then he said to Rai Sahib Munshi Ram, 'Remember, I have already taken a bath, so no bath is to be given to my body. And I have already changed into clean clothes. Please do not wait for anyone for my cremation and no memorial should be erected for me.' "

Maharaj Ji emphasized that saints go to great lengths to see that we are not tempted to turn our attention to external practices and rituals and, out of a false sense of loyalty and homage, start giving importance to stone mausoleums and 'samadhis'. The highest expression of loyalty to the memory of a saint is to follow the teachings to which he devoted his entire life, to follow the inward mystic path back to God. When we get entangled in these external forms of devotion, we gradually lose sight of the real teachings of the saints. Moved by sentiments and outward human emotions, we forget the inner reality. But it is to point out the mystic reality that saints take birth. It is love and devotion which are of importance, not any display of superficial devotion.

Maharaj Ji also gave an account of the Great Master's visit to Agra, the place where Soami Ji was born and started his satsang. During the course of his visit, some of the sevadars of Soami Bagh took him to see the samadhi of Soami Ji. But the Great Master regretfully told them that they had drifted away from Soami Ji's teachings. "You have put a string of razors around your neck." He commented, "Some day, it will cut your own throat." And today we can see the truth of that statement, for litigation began between the two Agra factions, Soami Bagh and Dayal Bagh, back in 1923, and over sixty years later, they are still fighting legal battles in the courts.

———

FIRST OFFICIAL VISIT TO AGRA

Right to Left—Shri Bhan Singh, Shri R.N. Mehta, Shri Daryailal Kapur, Captain Parshottam Singh Grewal, Maharaj Charan Singh, Shri Ahluwalia, H.H. Mehta Sahib, Shri Rao Sahib Shiv Dhayan Singh, Rai Sahib Munshi Ram, (next person not known), Shri S.S. Bhargava, Shri Sukhia (Secretary to H.H. Mehta Sahib)

Maharaj Ji's satsangs and visits to Agra

Maharaj Ji once mentioned that during his satsang visit to Agra in 1978, the members of the Dayal Bagh management called on him. Sondhi Sahib and other members of the Dera staff were also with Maharaj Ji on that trip.

During the course of their conversation, Maharaj Ji asked the Dayal Bagh members, when they (of the Soami Bagh) expected to finish the construction of Soami Ji's samadhi. Mr. Sukhia, a prominent member of their staff and a son-in-law of the late Mehta Sahibji Maharaj (their previous spiritual leader), replied that the same question had been put to B. Purshottam Das Tandon[1] many years earlier.

Mr. Sukhia said that in response to the question, Shri Tandon Ji had observed, "I wonder if it will ever be completed. It looks as if Soami Ji has just given an opportunity for the sangat to do seva."

Then Lalji Maharaj, the head of the Dayal Bagh institution at that time, said to Maharaj Ji, "If you (meaning the Radha Soami Satsang Beas) and we (Dayal Bagh) were given the right to worship the samadhi and were to participate in its construction, it could very soon be completed."

On hearing this, Maharaj Ji asked if the worship of Soami Ji's samadhi would be appropriate and

---

1. Shri Tandon was at that time the Chairman of Soami Bagh's Managing Committee. One-time president of the Indian National Congress, he was a greatly respected person in political and literary fields.

according to his teachings. But to this question, there was no reply from any of the members.

After the satsang, someone asked Maharaj Ji if he had ever visited Soami Bagh before. Maharaj Ji replied that he had previously visited Soami Bagh on three occasions.

The first time was back in 1945, soon after his marriage. He was on the way to visit his father-in-law's house at Pisawa, a village close to the town of Aligarh, near Agra. His brother was also posted at Agra, and Maharaj Ji wanted to visit him.

Since he was going to Agra, the Great Master asked him to call on Babuji Maharaj, who was the Master at Soami Bagh at that time. So Maharaj Ji, with his young bride, met Babuji Maharaj, who garlanded the new couple. He also inquired about the Great Master's well-being with considerable warmth and made arrangements for Maharaj Ji to see Soami Ji's samadhi, which then, as now, was still under construction. Babuji Maharaj was unable to take them himself, as he was very ill at that time.

The Great Master had also mentioned to Maharaj Ji that there were two small rooms which had been constructed by him in the lifetime of Baba Jaimal Singh Ji, and that Maharaj Ji should try to see them. Someone did point them out to him from a distance, but he was unable to actually visit them, in spite of his wish to do so.

His second visit to Agra was in 1948, when Maharaj Ji took Dr. Schmidt there, soon after the passing away of the Great Master. Rai Sahib

Munshi Ram had written to Mehta Sahib Ji, who was head of Dayal Bagh at that time, concerning Maharaj Ji's forthcoming visit. Arrangements were made for their stay at the guest house. This was natural, for Sardar Bahadur Ji, Rai Sahib Munshi Ram and Mehta Sahib Ji had been class fellows and friends during their college days.

Mehta Sahib Ji met Maharaj Ji and Dr. Schmidt with great warmth and affection, deputing his son-in-law, Mr. Sukhia, to take them around the educational institutions, the industrial plants and the whole campus of Dayal Bagh. In the evening, he hosted a dinner in their honour and introduced them both to members of his staff. He remembered the Great Master and Sardar Bahadur Ji with great love. This was Maharaj Ji's second visit.

Then, sometime after Maharaj Ji had come to the 'gaddi' in 1951, Rai Sahib Munshi Ram suggested that he should visit Agra, since this had been the place where Soami Ji had had his centre. This, then, was Maharaj Ji's third visit to the Soami Bagh and Dayal Bagh centres.

As this was an official visit—Maharaj Ji now being the head of Radha Soami Satsang Beas—a number of Dera staff members and prominent satsangis accompanied him. In fact, they were nine in number and advance intimation was given to Mehta Sahib Ji of their visit and of the number of people coming.

Arrangements for their stay were made at the guest house. However, one old satsangi, Sardar

Chanan Singh, insisted on accompanying them, making the party ten, instead of nine. On his arrival, Mehta Sahib Ji came to call on Maharaj Ji. Out of his usual courtesy, Maharaj Ji apologized to Mehta Sahib Ji for bringing along one extra guest. But much to everyone's surprise, the reply from Mehta Sahib Ji was, "You should not have brought him." Obviously, he was a very strict disciplinarian.

Maharaj Ji also wanted to attend satsang while he was there, but he was not informed of the time, nor invited to attend. So when he came to know that satsang was being held, he sent a message that he would like to attend it. Thereupon, he received an invitation and a chair was put out for him. Only shabds from *Sar Bachan* were recited in the satsang and Maharaj Ji noted that no elucidation of these shabds was given.

After being taken on a tour of the institution, Mehta Sahib Ji introduced his staff to Maharaj Ji and his party. Shri R. N. Mehta, a prominent satsangi from Delhi who was accompanying Maharaj Ji, then requested Mehta Sahib Ji to pose for one group photo. After one photograph had been taken, Mr. R. N. Mehta requested that they wait for one more, but Mehta Sahib Ji declined, such was his sense of discipline.

Maharaj Ji was surprised that none of his other acquaintances there came to meet him. Mr. Dinanath, for example, a retired police officer from the Punjab, was the security officer there, and he was well known to Maharaj Ji's father and uncle. But then, late in the night, he came to meet Maharaj Ji, arriving through the back door of the bathroom. He revealed that all the members of their staff had been given strict instructions not to meet Maharaj Ji.

Rai Sahib Munshi Ram used to say that Mehta Sahib Ji was a very honest and upright man. He was intelligent and greatly respected in his service days. But he certainly was a great disciplinarian.

During Maharaj Ji's visit to Agra, he took the opportunity of calling on the Chairman of Soami Bagh, Sri Daya Ram, who was very ill. He received Maharaj Ji with great respect. Indeed, all of them there had great respect and love for the Great Master, and were very appreciative of the immense work carried out by the Masters of the Radha Soami Satsang Beas in propagating the philosophy of Nam in the Punjab and elsewhere. Sri Daya Ram arranged for Maharaj Ji to hear the chanting of Soami Ji's shabds and he, in return, wanted to listen to the way in which shabds were recited in our satsangs. This was immediately arranged.

Maharaj Ji then said that their recitation was better than that of the Beas pathis.

At Soami Bagh, Maharaj Ji wanted to give some money in seva and after consultation with Rai Sahib Munshi Ram, a cheque for eleven hundred rupees was offered. The cheque, however, was returned with the remark that they did not accept cheques in seva. The seva should be sent in cash, but no receipt would be issued. So Maharaj Ji arranged for the correct amount to be sent in cash. And thus the visit was completed.

A few years later Mehta Sahib Ji sent to the Dera a copy of the judgement of the Supreme Court on one preliminary issue in the case which has been going on between Dayal Bagh and Soami Bagh for many years. The ramifications of the case are tortuous, but back in September 1923, Dayal Bagh had filed a suit against Soami Bagh, claiming the right to visit Soami Ji's samadhi for the purpose of worship. On some preliminary issues, the case has even gone to the Privy Council and now to the Supreme Court, but so far the suit has not been settled.

In his letter, Mehta Sahib Ji wanted to know how the Satguru was nominated at Beas. He wanted copies of the wills of the Great Master and Sardar Bahadur Ji, along with a copy of the Trust Deed of the Radha Soami Satsang Beas. All the documents were duly sent to him.

In his letter, Mehta Sahib Ji had also requested Radha Soami Satsang Beas to join in the construction of Soami Ji's samadhi, so that it could be rapidly completed.

Rai Sahib Munshi Ram replied that the Great Master was opposed to the building of a samadhi as it was not in conformity with the teachings of Soami Ji. Therefore, he said, Radha Soami Satsang Beas could not join them in this project.

Maharaj Ji's fourth visit to Agra was a historic occasion. It is said that Soami Ji had been asked by some of his disciples as to when he would again come in human form. He is said to have replied, "In a hundred years." And it was after a lapse of one hundred years, in November 1978, that Maharaj Ji went to Agra to hold satsang.

For many years, Bibi Rali had been suggesting to Maharaj Ji that he should hold satsang at Agra, the birthplace of Soami Ji. She had had a close association with Agra because, as a child, she had received initiation from Chacha Ji Maharaj, before she came with her father to stay at the Dera and serve the Great Master. She was then initiated by the Great Master.

So in 1978, to please Bhuaji (Bibi Rali) and to honour her wish, Maharaj Ji agreed to hold satsang at Agra. Accordingly, he asked Mr. R. N. Mehta to make the necessary arrangements. It was a colossal task, for satsangis from all parts of India were keen to attend this satsang—the very first to be held in this city after such a long time, and at the place where it all began.

However, with Maharaj Ji's infinite grace, the task was successfully accomplished, and a high degree of excellence was attained in making all the arrangements. In fact, the extent of the scale on which these arrangements were made created quite a sensation amongst the people of Agra.

Only the saints know how it is that they accomplish their work in this world. The seva performed on their behalf by their disciples is infused with a coherence and serenity which is difficult to describe. And the atmosphere of love lifts us out of our little selves into a greater awareness of the Master's presence.

The following account is taken from that given by Mr. S.L. Sondhi, Secretary of Radha Soami Satsang Beas:

"Maharaj Ji held three satsangs from the 24th of November 1978. His programme began with a visit to Soami Bagh where, as previously arranged, he arrived with his party at 3.45 p.m. on 24th November and was received very cordially and with due respect at the main entrance by the members of the administrative council. He was taken round the Bagh and shown those places which are held in great reverence by the mission.

"The first satsang was held at 5.00 p.m. on that day in the Paliwal park, adjacent to the Agra University campus.

"On the following day, Maharaj Ji called at Dayal Bagh where, as previously arranged, he arrived at 10.30 a.m. and was very cordially received by Rev. Lal Sahib Ji, the head of the mission, and members of his administrative council. At 12.15 p.m. Shri Agam Parshad Mathur, the head of the mission in Pipal Mandi, met Maharaj Ji. He was with Maharaj Ji for about half an hour. The second satsang was held in the evening at 5.00 p.m.

"On the third day, Rev. Lal Sahib Ji called on Maharaj Ji in the morning, accompanied by members of his council, remaining with him for about half an hour. After the meeting, Maharaj Ji proceeded to the pandal to deliver his third discourse, which lasted nearly two hours.

"For many of the people in the audience, the

satsangs must have been a deeply enlightening experience, for it is doubtful whether they had previously heard such a brilliant exposition of the teachings, set out so lucidly and forcefully, yet in such a simple style. The common man's reaction can best be judged from the following remarks made by a Soami Bagh satsangi after the last satsang. 'Is it not possible to have satsangs like these every day?' said he. When told that he would have to come to Beas to hear such satsangs, he queried, 'When will Maharaj Ji come to Agra again?'

"In the end, a word may be said about Mr. R. N. Mehta. He had to work under very trying conditions, and it must be said to his credit that he bore the brunt of his responsibility very cheerfully and willingly, having full faith in Maharaj Ji's grace to enable him to fulfil this most difficult assignment successfully."

Masters above prejudices of caste and creed

Prejudice takes different forms in different countries, and in India there has always been considerable mutual prejudice between Hindus and Muslims and between various castes. Nowadays it is somewhat less than previously, but it is still a significant factor in society. However, mystics who see God in everyone and everything are above such distinctions, as the following incidents illustrate.

Many years ago, on one of our visits to Sikanderpur, we were all with one accord praising Beji for the excellent cooking. The food was delicious and very well cooked. Beji said, "Do you know, our cook is a Muslim lady. She used to be with Maharaj Ji when he was at Sirsa, doing his cooking and looking after his house and domestic needs."

Hearing this, we became interested, asking her to tell us more of Maharaj Ji and how it had all happened, for at that time everyone was very conscious of caste and racial prejudice. And for a Muslim lady to be a cook in a Hindu or Sikh household was most unusual.

Beji said that from the beginning, Maharaj Ji had never felt any difference between Hindus and Muslims or between social castes. In fact, he had many Muslim friends during his college days.

After his marriage, he found that his wife, too, had no caste prejudice. She engaged a Muslim servant, whose name was Azim Hussain, from her parents' village of Pisawa. Maharaj Ji kept him in his house at Sirsa, naming him Mohan, so that when Maharaj Ji's family visited him they would not object. At that time, his family members were reluctant to engage servants from amongst Muslims and Harijans, though later on, due to Maharaj Ji's persuasion, they gradually accepted the idea. Now no one in the family has any such prejudice. For a considerable period of time, no one discovered that Maharaj Ji had a Muslim servant.

Then, when the Great Master became sick, Maharaj Ji came to stay with him and to serve him. As his wife was expecting a baby at the time, he sent her to Pisawa for her confinement and for the birth. So, being on his own, he used to have his meals with Bibi Rali at the Great Master's house.

There was, however, no servant to give him tea in bed, which was his habit, and he missed it. But somehow he found a sevadar boy, named Ratan, and he engaged him as a servant, and actually taught him how to make his tea. Later on Maharaj Ji found out that he was a Harijan, but to him this was of no importance.

After the Great Master had passed away, Maharaj Ji took Ratan with him to Sirsa, and he remained with Maharaj Ji for quite a few years. Now he is a prominent sevadar in the Delhi sangat.

Concerning the Muslim ladies, Beji told us that their stay began when the Great Master was in Amritsar for treatment, during the time of partition. There was tremendous communal unrest and rioting going on all around. As can be imagined, many of the satsangis from a Muslim background were unwilling to go to Pakistan from where they could not easily come for satsang and darshan. Even those who had no such ties were also naturally unhappy to leave the places which they knew as home. Two such village ladies were brought to the Great Master by some satsangis, requesting the Great Master to give them shelter.

By that time, the Great Master had received the

news from Pisawa that Maharaj Ji and his wife had been blessed with a baby girl. Accordingly, he called Maharaj Ji who was with him at Amritsar, asking him to take care of these ladies. He told Maharaj Ji that one would look after his house and kitchen and that the other would help to care for the baby. The Great Master then gave these ladies new Hindu names, so that no one would harass them.

Beji told us that one of the ladies looked after all three of his children and the other took care of the kitchen and domestic work at Sirsa, when Maharaj Ji was practising there as a lawyer. Then, when he moved to Sikanderpur to help manage the farm, Beji said, "I put her in charge of the entire kitchen." And she looked after the kitchen and all the cooking, until her death.

Even today, Maharaj Ji's personal, trusted and loyal servant is from the Harijans. Just recently Maharaj Ji came to know of it, after twenty years, for he never asked him his caste when he engaged him, not considering it a matter of any importance. He is a very intelligent person, looking after Maharaj Ji's needs and serving him extremely well. Maharaj Ji entrusts him with the care of his entire house.

Some sayings of Maharaj Ji

The following are a few of the Master's frequent sayings, taken mostly from his English meetings:

The Lord worships Himself through us.

Calculated humility is just like costume jewellery.

When the Lord is one and He is within us and we have all been made alike, naturally the path leading to Him cannot be different for different people. It is bound to be the same.

When He is within us, we may deceive others, even ourselves sometimes, but we cannot conceal anything from Him.

Money is a bliss and also a curse, at the same time.

A biting tongue (stinging words) pierces deeper than a sword thrust.

We would do better to judge ourselves first, than to judge others.

Love is losing your own identity, merging into the Beloved and becoming one with Him.

Faith is independent of reason.

Our critics are our best guide in life.

Use your words sparingly, if you wish them to be powerful.

Love and forgiveness heal the wounds of the heart.

Love, dramatized, loses its depth.

To blow a trumpet of your love is like displaying imitation flowers.

Love removes all obstacles on the path.

Love is beyond price.

Simplicity of nature is a sign of a saint.

It is easy to become a teacher but difficult to be a pupil.

Love rises in devotion, but falls down in passion.

Happiness lies in adjusting to the events of life, for events will never change.

Solitude is your best companion.

Separation from the Beloved is essential to know the depth of your love.

Life without humour is like a body without a soul.

I am with myself when I am alone.

One moment with Thee is worth more than a whole life without Thee. Life without Thee is meaningless.

Happiness lies more in loving than in being loved; in giving than in receiving; in serving than in being served; in forgiving rather than in being forgiven.

Man without character is like a flower without fragrance.

I never fail when I listen to myself but I fail if I ignore it.

My every fall is a step to my success.

True knowledge is to forget all that one has learnt.

Sensual pleasures cost much more than they are worth.

Do what you should, not what you can.

Loving, kind and sweet words are more precious than jewels.

Superior to all is the servant of all.

The world is a bridge. You can walk over it, but do not build on it.

He knows best.

_____

Maharaj Ji's humility

All those who have ever come in contact with Maharaj Ji, whether satsangis or non-satsangis, have always been impressed by his natural humility. His every gesture and action, in his thinking and during conversation, one is always impressed by this quality.

He is always the first to fold his hands and say "Radha Soami" to you, even before you greet him. And if anyone tries to put a garland around his neck, he prevents him. Even when one goes for an interview, no matter how much one tries to sit on the carpet in front of him, he always insists that one sits on a chair, at the same level as he is sitting.

Every morning when he goes to satsang, dressed in a simple white kurta, with a shawl draped elegantly around him in an inimitable style, he walks towards the dais and folds his hands in greeting to the sangat. Then, before anyone has realized it, he bows to the sangat.

This is a unique example of his humility, not to be seen or found anywhere else. Many newcomers, seeing this, are wonderstruck, for it is customary that in such congregations the audience bows first. Usually, the followers bow to their respected leader. It is not seen anywhere else, that the guru bows low to the gathered multitudes. In many gatherings, the leader or a famous personage enters the stage amidst glowing spotlights, to the rapturous and enthusiastic applause of his admirers. Standing there, he accepts the adulation for some time before greeting his audience. This is not so with the Masters.

A sadhu who once came to meet Maharaj Ji, on seeing him bow to him before he could himself bow, felt so overwhelmed by Maharaj Ji's humility that he asked him: "Whenever we go to saints or to religious leaders either for an interview or at a gathering, they expect us to bow to them. This is the usual custom. This is the only place where I have seen a Master bowing to the disciples first. Why is this so?"

Maharaj Ji replied, "I am the servant of the Lord and the Lord is in everyone."

In this brief reply was the answer not only to the question, but also the reason for his deep-rooted humility.

The salad incident

Maharaj Ji has always lived in this world with the deepest perception of how it functions, yet his unassuming nature is such that the world has never touched him.

Once, during one of the English meetings, Maharaj Ji narrated an interesting incident which happened to him on his first visit to Great Britain in 1962.

Colonel Sanders, who was Maharaj Ji's Representative there at the time, arranged a trip for himself, Maharaj Ji and his travelling companion, Professor Janak Puri, to Edinburgh, in Scotland. Whilst there, the colonel took them out to lunch at a vegetarian restaurant.

He assured Maharaj Ji that he had seen to the arrangements and that only pure vegetarian food would be served to them. He ordered the lunch and went to the toilet. Meanwhile, salad plates were brought and put on the table before Maharaj Ji and Professor Puri.

On looking at his salad, he noticed something white and yellow, with which he was unfamiliar, cut neatly into small slices and placed amongst the vegetables. So he asked the Professor, "Is it a vegetable or a fruit?"

They discussed it and thought that it must be some kind of vegetable which grew in Europe, but not in India, which would explain why they had never seen it before.

Anyhow, they awaited their host before com-
mencing their meal. When the colonel returned and
saw the salads, he exclaimed, "Oh my God! They
have mixed egg pieces in the salad." Then, apologiz-
ing profusely, he got the dish exchanged immediately.

Until then, Maharaj Ji had never seen an egg
(in slices) and for that reason had been unable to
recognize it. In fact, Maharaj Ji said that he had
never seen any non-vegetarian dish, not even meat
or wine of any kind, during his life.

There was no question of his having seen such
things during his protected childhood at the Dera,
nor even in his later life, as a student at the Law
College in Lahore. Even as a practising lawyer at
Sirsa, where he was a socially popular person and
an active member of the local club, he had never
seen eggs, meat or wine.

Living amongst everything in this world,
Maharaj Ji has always remained spotless and above
all, like a lotus flower on the surface of water,
holding open its petals to the pure sun above.

The Lord alone is the giver

Maharaj Ji related an anecdote in satsang the
other morning, which the Great Master used to tell.
He was talking about contentment. Contentment, he
said, is an attitude of the mind, and one has to learn
to keep the mind under control. If one gives a long

rope to the mind, there is no limit to one's desires.
Maharaj Ji illustrated this point with a story concerning Emperor Akbar.

Emperor Akbar was a great Moghul ruler in
India during the sixteenth century. One day whilst
hunting in the jungle he somehow became separated
from his retinue. Becoming extremely thirsty, he
began searching for water and, finding a farmer's
well, he asked the farmer for a drink of water. This
was readily provided and, in addition, with the
natural hospitality of simple country folk, the farmer
also served a meal to the hungry man, little realizing that his guest was the Emperor, for the king had
not disclosed his identity.

The king was very happy, and grateful to the
farmer for his hospitality. He then informed the
farmer that he was the king, and told him that if he
should ever be in need of anything, he had only to
come to him and ask. But the farmer replied that he
was just a simple man who tilled the land and gave
revenue to the king, so there was little that he
would need. Anyway, the king gave him his ring as
a remembrance, asking the farmer to bring it with
him to show to the palace guards, should he ever
require an audience.

Time passed and the farmer forgot about both
the king and the ring. Some years later, there
was a severe drought in the land, putting a great
strain upon the meagre resources of the poor
farmer. The farmer's wife reminded him of the
king and asked him, since they were in dire
straits, to go to him for help. So the farmer went to

Agra, which was Akbar's capital, taking the ring with him.

When the farmer reached the king's palace at Agra he showed the king's ring to the guards and was soon ushered into the presence of the king. But Akbar was praying, so the farmer quietly went and stood near him.

Akbar was relating all his troubles and woes to the Lord. "O Lord," he was saying, "because of this drought there will be little revenue and the coffers in the treasury will become empty. Then how shall I pay salaries to the army? How will I even feed them? How will I take proper care of my harem? And what will happen to all my royal pageantry and splendour? How will I administer my kingdom without any money?" The king was in great misery, and was praying to the Lord to solve his problems.

The farmer, after listening quietly and hearing all this, began to turn away and leave without meeting the king. But Akbar, on finishing his prayers, happened to see the man and, recognizing in him the farmer in whose debt he was, called him back.

The king asked the farmer why he was turning away without meeting him and without making any demands. The farmer replied, "O King, I had come to ask for your help in my difficulties, but having heard *your* problems and the great demands *you* were making on the Lord, I changed my mind. I had thought that you were really a king, capable of giving anything. But I find that you are a greater beggar than I! If I have to ask for anything, I will ask of Him only and knock at His door."

Maharaj Ji then said that the bigger the man, the bigger are his problems, desires and demands—and his discontent and unhappiness are also correspondingly increased. One of the greatest Indian emperors, Akbar the Great, was an extremely discontented man, while the poor farmer was far more contented and happy than he.

Maharaj Ji then quoted Kabir, who said, "The king of kings is the one who has no needs."

(ਜਿਸ ਕੋ ਕਛੁ ਨ ਚਾਹੀਏ ਸੋਈ ਸ਼ਹਿਨਸ਼ਾਹ)

And in this context, Maharaj Ji often says, "To ask for anything else but you, is to ask for more and more sorrows."

(ਵਿਣੁ ਤੁਧੁ ਹੋਰੁ ਜਿ ਮੰਗਣਾ ਸਿਰਿ ਦੁਖਾ ਕੈ ਦੁਖ)

Veiled hints

Another incident was related by one of Maharaj Ji's friends, regarding the way in which he always tries to help by hinting about any coming disaster. He said that if we could only take his advice seriously, so much calamity could be avoided. Yet we take his advice lightly and mostly never pay any heed to it until the incident occurs. Then we realize how foolish we have been. The events are described just as the friend narrated them.

"Whilst visiting our home on one occasion, Maharaj Ji advised my wife, 'Behenji, please attend to your simran regularly for the next thirty days.'

"But she replied jokingly, 'You do it for me,' because we had known Maharaj Ji for ten years before he became the Master, and he was always like a family member to us, afterwards keeping up the same relationship.

"Again whilst sitting in the car when he was about to leave, he emphatically told my wife that she must attend to her simran. But she did not take the advice seriously and never did it.

"Some time later, we had to leave our home in order to attend a marriage at Simla. After four days had passed, we received a trunk call from a neighbour, stating that there had been a theft in our home, committed by our servant. We returned that evening and found that all our valuables had been stolen. We informed the police and then wrote a letter to Maharaj Ji. But before he could receive it, a letter arrived from him in which he mentioned that he knew what had happened.

"After a few days he came to visit us and said to my wife, 'I had asked you to attend to your simran, but you did not do it. Now, just forget whatever your servant has taken from you and be grateful to the Lord for what is left behind, as this is still sufficient for your needs.'

"I said, 'Maharaj Ji she was expecting sympathy from you!'

"Maharaj Ji replied, 'I am sympathizing with her,

as so much has been left!' Everyone laughed and, by his grace, we took the whole incident lightly."

Excerpts from Maharaj Ji's letters

The following are extracts from Maharaj Ji's personal letters to friends and relatives. They were written in his own hand. These extracts indicate that in spite of his high spiritual level, he still maintains the same human relationship with his friends as before, not letting them feel any difference in any way in his dealing with them. On the contrary, he always remains the most loving and caring of friends.

April 16th, 1953, Dera

". . . On my arrival I found an American couple waiting for me. Yesterday they were discussing Sant Mat with me the whole day. Americans seem to be tired of their material progress and are in search of peace and truth now. I am glad I have been able to satisfy them.

"The more I realize that I am not worthy of the job I am holding, the more it seems to create faith in them. Their love and confidence hardly let me think about myself dispassionately. . . ."

November 6th, 1957

"As fixed up we left Delhi on 1st November by the G. T. Express and reached Jabalpur on the next day at 3 p. m. . . You cannot imagine the crowd at the railway station. . . . Only with great effort could I reach my car. . . .

". . . The gathering was about ten thousand in the satsang and they all heard it in pin drop silence. You will find from my programme that at night I am in the train and during the day I have to hold two satsangs. If you just care to place before you the railway map, you will just know as to what I am going through. Now I know with what difficulties and from what distances people come to Beas. Their eyes are full of tears of love and affection. How I wish that I be worthy of all that they show and do to me. . . ."

***

May 8th, 1960, District Kangra

"You will be shocked to know that brother Clair shot himself dead on the 6th morning, in his house compound. There was some tube-well enquiry against Mr. Rarewala, and Mr. Clair was unnecessarily harassed concerning that. As you know he was very honest and straightforward, he just could not bear this blackmailing. It is a good slap on the face of the politicians,

if they have any heart to feel. Poor Pritam and
her children—you just cannot bear to see them
crying and weeping. You know what this
tragedy means to me. Pritam immediately sent
word to me here at Bahota, a place about 60
miles from Nangal. I hastened to join them to
attend the last rites and have come back here
again to resume my satsang tour. . . . Mr. Clair
has left a will declaring me as legal guardian
for his children. Another burden on my feeble
shoulders. . . ."

***

December 24th, 1960

"Life is so simple but we people create so
many problems and complications, that we
spend the whole of our life in solving them. Do
not know when we are going to learn to take
simple things in a simple way."

***

May 9th, 1961

"You will be sorry to know that at Ludhiana I met with a serious accident, but by
Maharaj Ji's grace Damodar[1] and myself both
escaped.

"At Ludhiana railway crossing when we
were waiting for the railway gate to open,

---

1. His driver.

suddenly, on opening the gate, a cart full of iron bars about 6 inches round and 35 feet in length pierced the front screen, just passing by Damodar, and reaching where I was sitting on the back seat. When the bars were just one inch away from my head, the cart stopped. There were three to four thousand people there and everybody was surprised how we had escaped death.

"By Maharaj Ji's grace, I was so calm and cool that I even laughed when all was over. The iron bars went 6 feet inside the car and they were spread about 3 feet apart.

"At the time of the accident, I was doing simran as a matter of habit. Then it took us two hours with the police for the formalities. . . .

"Everybody here at home and in Dera is feeling very nervous about this trip of mine abroad, especially when Mehta[1] is not keeping well.

"Maharaj Ji is always with me and I have no fear whatsoever. I hardly need anybody else's protecting hand."

***

May 28th, 1961, Manila

". . . Against my expectations this has turned out to be just a satsang tour. I have to hold satsang everywhere I go, and every day.

---

1. Who was to accompany him.

Even before my arrival they give my picture
and satsang programme to all the local papers
and then I am bound down. . . . They are just
killing us by kindness. . . . Every place has its
own beauty, its own culture and dress. . . . I am
giving two satsangs in the local Gurdwara.
Sindhi and Punjabi brothers I find everywhere I
go and both understand my language. They very
much appreciate the satsangs and are surprised
when no appeal is made for collections. Anyway it is a wonderful trip and I am becoming
quite rich in experience. . . ."

***

June 28th, 1961, from on board ship

". . . I had been very busy . . . holding
satsang everywhere—attending so many recep-
tions. . . . By Maharaj Ji's grace, I get facilities
of all types wherever I go. I meet satsangis
everywhere and then I get so many admirers
everywhere after satsang. It is really a pleasure
to meet all types of people and to have various
types of discussions. This trip is not a rest in
the real sense, rather I am quite exhausted and
tired.

"I am lucky to have a place on this ship.
This is another experience I never had before.
On the ship you have a world of your own—
quite unconcerned with what is happening outside.

". . . I travelled quite incognito till Saigon, but there someone brought a newspaper which had my photo, as interviewed by the press. Now everybody is anxious to discuss religion and it is amazing what a poor knowledge people have of their own faith. Mostly there are French on the boat. . . . I think the most wonderful time I have had during this trip is surely the period I am spending on the boat."

***

May 24th, 1967

"I have bad news to share. The financial company where I have invested about Rs.50,000/- in the names of my different family members has collapsed.

". . . Do not worry about me. Maharaj Ji has given me sufficient strength to pull through all that and he has also given us all sufficient to go through this life. I am just writing to warn you about the situation. . . ."

***

July 15th, 1967

". . . I know he has a good heart and a bad temper, and on top of all is very sensitive. . . . His heart is still in India. He is fighting very hard with himself, and his emotions pile up from day to day. . . . It is only you who have to rise to the occasion and pacify him and explain everything with love, when he is in a better mood to hear. He has to fight his battle all alone without any help and support from his parents, so his mood is natural. Within himself he is terribly missing me, especially when I cannot meet him at the same level due to the strange role my destiny has allotted me to play.

"I will also write to him to learn to control his temper. He feels it—does his best, but just cannot help this. Both of you . . . should live in love. I will also try to straighten him up here and there. . . ."

***

June 2nd, 1968, Singapore

". . . My whole trip is just wonderful and it cannot be described in words. People are so loving and kind and doing their best to make my stay pleasant everywhere. I do not remember having done anything in this life to deserve so much of their love. They receive me with a smile and their eyes are full of loving tears at my departure. People are very receptive to satsang. I cannot describe Maharaj Ji's grace and blessings on me. . . ."

***

June 26th, 1973, Bangalore

". . . I love this solitude and peace and not being haunted by any visitors. Life is so simple

and beautiful to live, provided one can rise
above these human failings. They always keep
one entangled in the net of worry and misery.
Whatever has to happen, has already happened
and we human mortals are just helpless specta-
tors. If we can just withdraw this 'self', then
only can we enjoy this drama of life. I mean to
give no sermon, I am just in a mood to pour
out. . . ."

***

July 19th, 1988

". . . I am quite conscious of your physical, economic and emotional life-long struggle,
but I can't help admiring and appreciating the
way you have gone through all this smilingly.
As a satsangi you are well aware that we are
here to go through our individual destiny, and
no one can change the events of our life. Now
this depends on the attitude of our mind, as to
how we go through the ups and downs or the
events of this life without losing our balance, or
spend our life in agony. . . .

"When you started taking liberty with your
diet and compromising with the basic principles
of Sant Mat, it terribly pained me, as I knew its
consequences, but I never said anything to you
about it lest I may hurt you. I am glad at least
you kept love and faith alive in yourself and
never missed an opportunity to attend satsang. I
assure you this is helping you to a great extent.

MAHARAJ JI AND LOUISE HILGER

I have great faith in Him that ultimately He will forgive you for your past and will take you into His fold forever.

"For the last three or four months you were insisting to know from me as to why you have to suffer so much, though all through you were conscious within yourself of its cause. . . . I am glad ultimately you yourself realized it and took a bold step, and have reverted back to the Sant Mat way of life. Be strict with yourself, and I assure you, you will never have to repent for this.

"You were very lucky to find such a gentle, kindhearted and helpful man in your husband. Normally man, by nature, is selfish. The wife or any woman is not his priority. He needs her, but doesn't want to be possessed. On the other hand, for a woman, man is her whole existence. Woman has to create that much understanding in herself to live happily with a man. . . .

"Please just forget whatever has happened and have faith in him. There is no limit to His Grace, and His protecting hand and my good wishes and prayers are always with you. . . ."

Louise Hilger

Miss Louise Hilger is a well-known and devoted initiate of the Great Master. Coming from the U.S.A., she is now permanently settled at the Dera. There is no English book published by the Radha Soami Satsang Beas which has not been scrutinised by her searching eyes. She is a great asset to the Dera Publications Department. Right from the beginning of Maharaj Ji's time, in 1952, she has also been working as a private and personal secretary to Maharaj Ji. For the first few years she used to visit the Dera for six months every year, and now for the last many years she has been living here permanently.

Maharaj Ji often says, "She is my seniormost staff member—even senior to myself, in the sense that she was here when Sardar Bahadur Ji died and was cremated—a painful privilege which was denied to me."

With Maharaj Ji's permission, I have taken the following extracts from her file of Maharaj Ji's personal and private correspondence with his friends and relatives. These letters tell us much more about his thoughts and feelings. They also contain much sound advice on dealing with the problems of life.

A few excerpts from letters from Maharaj Ji's personal file

August 19th, 1965

". . . Destiny has assigned to me a very unusual role to play. I am always surrounded by the people who love me, and am thrown away from the ones whom I adore. Whatever I may carry within myself, I must laugh and proclaim that I am happy. This is supposed to go with my office. . . . I must console and look after others. When I am happy, I must weep with them and when I am sad, I must laugh with them. . . ."

September 19th, 1965

". . . You hear on the BBC whatever we are facing here on the border. We are, till yet, absolutely safe due to Maharaj Ji's grace. They are trying to bombard the Beas railway station and road bridge and also the ammunition depot just in front of Dera. Bombs fall right and left without hitting any target. People are not the least nervous. India seems to have the upper hand in the battle. The same India, the same nation, is at war with itself (India and Pakistan)—what a shame! It was a folly to partition the country at the time of independence. Some day they will both realize this. . . .

"Do not worry about us. We could get shelter in no better fort than Dera. Maharaj Ji's protecting hand is on us all. . . ."

***

June 10th, 1968

". . . Often I feel that I am with my old self, but then I miss that company and sometimes feel

quite tortured. Being always surrounded with so
much love and kindness, it is strange that I am still
not there. . . ."

***

October 24th, 1972

". . . I can well understand how lonely you
must be feeling. . . . But if you look at it from a
different angle, you should be happy that you at
least get time for yourself and can live with yourself for some time in peace and tranquillity.

"To be alone, especially when one is so used to
family life, is a very rare privilege and opportunity.
One can reflect and look within. Then we see how
much we are attached unnecessarily to the people all
around and how we just try to deceive ourselves
that we belong to someone or someone belongs to
us. The realization that we are alone and nothing in
this world belongs to us is a great boon and grace
of the Father. Then, naturally, one looks to Him for
guidance and help to overcome this loneliness,
which ultimately is our goal.

". . . Still, I am not lucky enough to be alone,
as I am always surrounded by satsang activities or
by friends and family members. Anyway, I have to
make the best use of the bargain and be happy with
myself. . . . I have given myself entirely to the duty
and cause which has been thrust upon my shoulders
and, in my own humble way, am doing my best to
attend to it. All the same, I am quite grateful to

Him for giving me so much strength to go through this routine and face the ups and downs of the administration.

"This recent tour to Delhi is the first time I have left the Dera for six months. Though mostly I have been confined to my bed, I have never worked so hard for the administration of Dera, nor taken so much interest in its routine affairs as I did during those six months from my bed.

"The income tax laws are changing every year. Having made a Society and Trust, we always have to be alert so that we may not be caught napping. By His grace, people are very helpful and sympathetic, and I am very fortunate to have a loyal and devoted team of staff members to help me go through this administration and routine.

"Sometimes, no doubt, I am pulled by my responsibilities of a husband and father towards my wife and children, but then I know that by myself I can do nothing as everything is in the hands of Maharaj Ji. You know that the land ceiling law has been enforced recently. That means cutting a major slice from the landed property held by us. But, as you know, it is not the land which is yielding any income or sustaining us. It is only His grace which has given us everything, and is helping us pull through this life with certain comfort, convenience and standard. So, I am not much concerned about what is happening. . . ."

***

November 4th, 1977

". . . Our guest house is full of foreigners from practically all nationalities, and they keep me quite occupied with their personal problems, interviews and evening meetings. My duties start early in the morning at about 3.30 – 4.00 o'clock and end up to 10.00 at night. Except for one hour's break after lunch, I am always on my toes, running about, attending to people. Unfortunately, there is no 'Sunday' for me and the question of a holiday does not arise.

"You will be surprised to know that today I have completed 26 years in this office and I am finding it very hard to believe that I have been able to pull through all this—and yet I am here, attending to your letters. In law, if anybody is sentenced to life-imprisonment, he is paroled after twelve to fourteen years; but in Sant Mat, a life-sentence means, until death takes pity on you. Anyway I am going through my duties and I have no regrets, but I am grateful for His grace and help. I am keeping reasonably good health for my age, but I often get tired. Perhaps this may now be the effect of age. Thanks to His grace I have no family problems and neither any economic ones. . . ."

***

March 6th, 1978

". . . We all thoroughly enjoyed this Rajasthan trip, though I had been to every place before, but previously with so much company. This time it was just a little different. No matter how many times one sees these historic places, they have their own charm and beauty. . . .

"Sometimes one wonders and is amazed how these princes could build such palatial forts and lead such luxurious lives, while the poor masses were starving and hardly living in huts. At the same time, one also pities them that, after having lived such luxurious lives, through what hardships they must be going now. Places where even a fly could not enter, now are swarmed by masses and have become public museums.

"I liked most my visit to Jaisalmer, where very few people go. It is right in the desert, on the border of Pakistan. The whole city is built in yellow stone. It is something unique to see a little town in the heart of the desert. It is yet to be invaded by civilization, and people are still living in their old style and simplicity. I know the prince personally. . . . I sometimes wonder how he could have reached this city when there used to be no rail or road connection from Jodhpur, which is about 250 km. from that place. . . .

". . . Then had to go to Jammu for the 4th and 5th. On the 5th morning, it rained very heavily, and the satsang had to be held in the rain. There was a gathering of about 50,000 people. But imagine, not a single one moved, and satsang went on right in the rain for more than an hour. People were drenched and sitting in mud, shivering (as it had also turned cold), but their faces were full of love

and devotion. They were quite unconscious of this
hardship caused by the rain. . . ."

***

April 5th, 1978

". . . When I reflect on my sense of duty, I
feel happy that I did not plan to go abroad this
year, but when I look to myself, I feel miserable
that I should be a prisoner of my responsibilities.
One can hardly rest and relax here as no matter
whether Dera is full or vacant, my daily routine is
practically the same. . . ."

***

September 18th, 1978

". . . Can you imagine, the attendance in
satsang at Poona was about 30,000 people. And I
remember when first I went, there were only twelve
people when I held satsang at Koregaun Park, at his
Highness Sangli's house—and practically all of them
were his family members or his secretarial staff.

I have not been too well for the last three
weeks, due to cough and cold, but now I am on
sulfa drugs and hope to be all right within a few
days. My problem is that I have to plan my satsang
long before and then I must go through with it,
whether I keep well or not, as cancellation means a
great hardship to many thousands of people. . . ."

***

November 2nd, 1978

". . . He is terribly shaken. His wife left for Delhi and she is still with her parents. He is all alone and I am trying to keep him with me as much as I can and am even taking him along with me on my tours. We all feel that we are not much attached to our children, but when the opportunity comes, then we realize how deep our roots and love are with them.

". . . You will be pleased to know that I am holding satsang for the first time at Agra on 24th, 25th and 26th November. It has been weighing on my mind that the source from where spirituality started in this faith is somehow drying up. Anyway, after a lot of deliberation and contemplation I have decided to hold satsang there. . . ."

***

December 15th, 1978

". . . I am glad he got to join me on the Agra trip, though for a brief period. It was an historic satsang tour, which I undertook after a lot of thinking and deliberation, as my predecessors never held any satsang there. I had a strong pull for the last so many years to hold satsang there, from where this whole 'spring of spirituality' was started by Soami Ji.

"I have been hearing all sorts of tales and rumours that both sister institutions there are drifting away from the real teachings and have given themselves to rituals and ceremonies, forgetting the core of Soami Ji's teachings. I couldn't resist the pull, so I kept the satsang tour. I am glad I got cooperation from everyone, and everyone was so kind and nice—rather helpful.

"No doubt they were quite nervous too, as they are unnecessarily thinking and giving meaning to our visit. We had no other intention than to pay our respect to that land, which has given us so much to grow and grow, and to remain in the service of the Father. . . ."

***

July 26th, 1979

". . . I really enjoyed my trip to Moscow and Leningrad. My host, Mr. Gujral, our Ambassador, a very fine and kind gentleman, looked after us very well, and made all arrangements for our tour. Moscow is a beautiful city. The roads are very wide, neat and clean, and the people are exceedingly disciplined. I had a very wrong notion about Russia, and I think my views are quite changed now.

"Their Metros (underground trains) are perhaps the best in the world. The floors (of the platforms) are very beautiful, made of marble and high quality chips; there were beautiful chandeliers hanging all around and the whole complex was spotlessly clean. It was very quiet in spite of thousands of people moving about. They seem to have solved a lot of problems of the masses.

"I was especially invited by church authorities to show me their churches. There is a beautiful monastery thirty or forty kilometres out of Moscow, also a theological seminary. Fortunately, there was Saint Peter's mass that day, so I could see the churches full of devotees attending the mass with dignity and devotion. They took me all around and somehow came to know about my religious context. We exchanged views very frankly on the Bible. The next day I was asked to call on the head of the Russian Orthodox Church, and he was good enough to present me with long-playing records of their church music and many books.

"I like Leningrad more than Moscow, especially the Hermitage Museum, which has huge collections of sculptures and paintings right from the time of Peter the Great. There was no problem of food anywhere, as a vegetable plate could always be available in the hotel. . . ."

***

May 21st, 1980

". . . I have been very busy since the April Bhandara—first, initiating at Delhi . . . then my photographic enterprise to Ujjain to attend the Kumbh Fair.[1] It was to be seen to believe how people are exploited in the name of religion—that even in the twentieth century people are living in such superstitions and ignorance, and just ritual and

---

1. An enormous religious festival held every twelve years.

ceremony is the be-all and end-all of their God-realization. Anyway, from the photographic point of view it was a paradise to see thousands of men and women taking bath in dirty water and moving about practically naked—especially the men rubbing ashes on their body and getting obeisance from the masses. . . ."

***

March 22nd, 1984

". . . The situation in the Punjab seems to find no end to the tension all around. Thanks to His grace we are quite peaceful here in the Colony, though everybody realizes that all of us are sitting on a volcano. . . .

"It is a pity that people hate and cut one another's throat in the name of religion, which should rather fill them with love and devotion for the Lord, and make them loving and kindhearted. This is what happens when we forget the real teachings of mystics and unnecessarily arrest them in some rigid organization and give it a shape of a religion or a cult. Religion should make us at least human, if not divine.

"Well! You know in what direction they are leading us today. Whenever a paid priest comes in to expound the teachings of any mystic or saint, these differences are bound to occur. The people are exploited and persecuted in the name of religion. The priests and politicians are more interested in their ego and in filling their pockets rather than trying to know, understand and follow the teachings of the mystics and saints. . . . Anyway, we are all quite safe here.

"It is very shameful what has happened in Haryana, but then this was boiling since long and you well know who can be held responsible for creating that tension and atmosphere there. . . ."

***

April 25th, 1984

". . . Due to the Punjab situation I cannot leave the Colony—not even for a day to visit my farm at Sikanderpur. . . . We are peacefully and comfortably sitting on a volcano."

***

May 14th, 1984

". . . The situation in the Punjab is horrible and is going from bad to worse every day. Shooting is going on all around, but by His grace it is calm, peaceful and quiet in the Colony, and we are doing our best to preserve it. It is surprising that in spite of all this, the attendance in satsang is becoming more and more every day, and now our Sankrant and Sunday satsangs are just like mini-bhandaras. . . ."

***

August 29th, 1984

". . . Infatuation, say love, brought you together in the bond of marriage . . . and the Lord has been merciful to bless you with two beautiful sons. Ups and downs or even storms sometimes do come in perhaps every marriage, as it is natural that the infatuation slowly and slowly fades out, and we start drifting away from each other. Love alone is not the only factor which should keep you together; but also the responsibility you have undertaken together to bring up your children, and the promise you have made before the Lord to pull through this together. You are both educated and mature persons, and I do hope you will rise to the occasion to create harmony and understanding. . . .

"I am not aware of the basic differences both of you can have between you, but basically and individually you are both very sweet and loving persons, and it should not be difficult for you to be happy with each other. Happiness lies in adjusting and giving yourself to each other, and not in hurting each other. One has to eschew one's false pride and rise above embarrassment in order to come closer and closer and live in harmony and peace, and discharge one's responsibility to the children. It is for you to win each other's confidence and love, and make a happy home, especially when marriage was your own choice.

"I don't want to look like a marriage counsellor, but my concern about your married welfare is very obvious. It is only a question of understanding each other, forgetting the past, starting anew and reaching one's emotional heights, to feel emotional security in each other. A husband, being the senior partner in this alliance, has perhaps more to adjust and sacrifice in order to have a happy atmosphere in the home. . . ."

***

July 11th, 1987

". . . I do not know what is going to become of this beloved province. It is a shame to see people shedding blood where so many saints and Gurus filled people with love and devotion for the Father, and brought humanity near to one another. Anyway, by Maharaj Ji's grace, all is well within the Colony and in the Hospital at Beas. . . ."

***

September 14th, 1989

". . . This is an age when we look back and start counting His blessings and look around at others and thank the Lord as to how gracious He has been to us, and this leaves us with no regrets in life at all. I am glad destiny is in His Hands, and He manoeuvres as it suits Him. Otherwise, left to ourselves, I wonder what a mess we would have made of our lives. . . ."

———

**Advice by Maharaj Ji
during satsang at Delhi
on November 25, 1989**

"In our modern civilization, we have made phenomenal progress in every sphere of life. Agriculture, engineering, medicine, defence, science— there is no phase of life in which we have not taken great strides. But when the mystics feel sorry for us and tell us that the world is drifting in an unfortunate direction, we wonder, 'Why do the saints not appreciate our modern civilization, our progress and all our multifarious developments?'

"Let us, therefore, look at ourselves and see whether we are happier than we were before, whether we have become healthier, more composed and contented, or whether we have become more miserable, and our desires, appetites and longings have increased.

"In the past we had so little, but we were contented. Now we have so much, and still we want more and more. Today, there are more diseases, more broken homes, more cases of mental tension and suicide, more hospitals are full of cancer patients.

"In olden days, we lived in thatched huts—all our family and children living in just one or two huts. We used to till the fields with our own hands or plough them with the help of bullocks. Marriages were arranged within the community, and our whole world was encompassed within a radius of fifteen or twenty miles. Within this range, we spent our entire life.

"Today, we have made great scientific progress. New medicines have been introduced, well-qualified physicians and surgeons are available; numerous courts of justice have been set up, so that we can even fight a law suit up to the Supreme Court, with adroit lawyers being there to help us.

"Why then do the mystics say that we have not advanced, that we are unhappy? Every type of facility is available to us, in every walk of life; then how can we be unhappy? Either there is something wrong in our thinking or in the viewpoint of the mystics.

"When we used to dwell in hutments, the entire family lived in close proximity. The family members would work all day, and in the evening they would have their meals together. They would have love and regard for one another; they would join together in rejoicing: in beating drums, in singing and in dancing. Then, fully relaxed, they would sleep in peace.

"Nowadays, we have large and beautiful mansions. Our rooms are air-conditioned; T.V. provides us with entertainment; telephones are at hand to enable us to communicate with others. And our beds are provided with good springs or with six-inch thick foam rubber mattresses. But even then we are unable to get a good night's sleep. We have to resort to tranquillizers and hypnosis, even to injections, to enable us to get some sleep. In the morning, we rise from bed, tense and tired, with a heavy head and aching joints.

"As for families, children used to have great respect for their parents, and they likewise loved their children. But today, parents return from their parties late at night, after the children have already gone to bed. Then they get up late in the morning long after the children have got up and left for school. Children's love and regard for their parents are naturally conditioned by their parents' preoccupations. So how can such children grow up to become a source of help and support to their parents? How can they have respect and affection for them?

"In earlier times, there used to be one physician or surgeon in a village, giving treatment to the ailing. He used to be an ordinary doctor, but every sick person was attended to, and at least everybody could get medicines.

"It is true that medical science has made extraordinary progress today. But just look at new ailments that are cropping up all the time, because the liberal use of chemicals in the production and preservation of food has an adverse effect on our body. And how many people actually get the benefit of doctors? How many get a bed in a hospital? Even if they are fortunate enough to get them, look at the huge expenses they incur for consultations and treatment. And, in many countries, the number of patients is so large that numerous sick people are seen lying on hospital verandahs.

"Again, there is no doubt that we produce enormous quantities of foodgrains today, but the prices are exorbitant. How can a poor man buy sugar at the rate of twelve or thirteen rupees per kilogram? How can he subsist and support his children with the high prices of food? It is not that there is any shortage of food in the world, but there is something wrong with our system of supply and distribution. The saints compassionately tell us that the rich cannot eat, because they are unable to digest the food, and the poor cannot obtain food because of the high prices! Who, then, has benefited from the huge quantity of food that is produced?

"Today you can file a law suit in the courts, but then there is no decision before the lapse of fifteen or even twenty years. The judges may be very competent and lawyers skilled, but no one gets an early decision.

"Today, new medicines are almost daily being introduced; intelligent and able doctors are there to administer them, but how many people really get the benefit of such treatment? Again, we have erected multi-storey buildings, palaces and mansions, yet see how many people pass their nights on pavements.

"So either there is something basically wrong with all this development, or with the way we are using it.

"Today, you marry according to your own choice, yet every third or fourth year you are in the law courts seeking a divorce. In olden days,

parents played a major role in arranging marriages. Though a little rough weather did come in
married life, the parents or elders of both parties
used to get together. They mediated and resolved the
differences, and the threatening storm would fade
away. Today parents do not know when their sons
or daughters have obtained a divorce, and when
they have married again. So who has gained from
all this progress?

"Ask anybody and you will find that he has no
time. The labourer has no time; the engineer has no
time; the doctor has no time; the industrialist has no
time. Who has time to relax? Who has some
moments of leisure? No one.

"What, then, have we gained from all this
progress, from all these developments? We cannot
find an hour for ourselves, not even half an hour
in which to relax. Everybody is suffering from
mental tension—every face reflects tension—no one
appears to be relaxed. Four people cannot sit
together and shake off their tension in laughter and
relaxation.

"The result is increasing incidence of heart
disease, diabetes and high blood pressure. Our
entire life has become artificial. We have forgotten
how to laugh, and how to shed tears. Our smiles
have become artificial, our tears have become
artificial.

"This is not entirely the fault of development.
We have become prisoners of the things that development and progress have given us. These things

were meant for our benefit, for our use; we were not meant for their benefit, for their use. But we have become slaves of the machinery, not its owners. We are possessed by it; we do not possess it. We should become the owners, the masters of all this progress. Every person should get enough food, should have shelter over his head, should be relaxed, should be free from tension. There should be no tension on anyone's mind.

"Parents should be loving towards their children, and children should have respect for their parents. These are the values which every human being cherishes in life. These are the basic values of life. If the values of life are lost, then what is the advantage of all this development? What is the benefit of all this progress?

"I am not against modern developments and the present civilization. But at no cost should we compromise with the basic values of human life. There should be leisure for us. We should lead a simple, relaxed and tension-free life. There should be unity and peace in the family, respect for our elders, and we should look after our children. Our food and environment should be healthy. We should be sympathetic and helpful to others. Our developments should lead us in this direction."

PART II

**Maharaj Ji's speech
on the Great Master's birthday
July, 1952**

You all know, today is the birthday of Huzur Maharaj Ji.

The days on which saints incarnate in this world are extremely happy and fortunate days for us, because their coming augurs the emancipation of millions of souls. The saints teach us the method of devotion, and, helping us to practise it, they carry us along with themselves to the lap of the Supreme Father. Thus we are released from the bonds of birth and death.

The birthdays of saints and mystics should not be celebrated merely by eating cakes and sweets; rather, we should look within ourselves and reflect over their message, over the divine path they bid us to adopt. We should search within, whether we are truly following their directions, whether we are steadfast on the path that they showed us, whether we are firmly adhering to the high principles of living they laid down for us. If there are shortcomings, then we should earnestly resolve to overcome them.

Saints come to the world not to lay the foundation of a new creed or religion. They come to dispel our illusions, to free us from our shackles of external practices, rituals and ceremonies. They come to impart to us the secret of Nam or Shabd, to teach us the method of meditation, to lead us back to our original Home, to the Lord.

It is we who, after the departure of such great mystics, distort and arrest their teachings so as to give them the shape of a formal religion. But the saints always come to herald the practice of Nam, to impart the secret of the divine Word to the true seekers of the Lord.

You all know, Huzur Maharaj Ji for 45 years promoted the message of Sant Mat in spite of all odds and obstacles, not caring for criticism from orthodox people; how he travelled to far-off places, from village to village, undergoing all sorts of hardship, even at that age. As a result of his loving efforts and untiring dedication, today we find his blessed devotees not only in all the corners of India, but also spread out in so many foreign countries. They, too, celebrate this day with love and gratitude.

College days

In one of the English meetings someone asked Maharaj Ji, "Did you do bhajan in your college days?" Maharaj Ji replied, "Let me tell you in confidence: I did it only casually, except for 60 days when I did it regularly. In 1936, when I was studying in Intermediate,[1] I was engaged but did not want to marry the girl I was engaged to. I went to Bhua Ji (Bibi Rali) and requested her to convey to

---

1. This is equivalent to the eleventh and twelfth grade.

the Great Master that I did not want to marry; my engagement should be broken. So when Bhua Ji mentioned it to the Great Master, he laughed and did not give it a thought. She pleaded many times, but nothing happened.

"In 1941, when I was in Law College, Bhua Ji again pleaded for me very strongly. The Great Master said, 'Well, I will break the engagement if he (Maharaj Ji) sits regularly in bhajan for one hour for sixty days.' So I sat regularly. When the sixty days were over, I came to Bhua Ji and told her, 'I have obeyed the Great Master explicitly. Now, please remind him of his promise.' Bhua Ji smilingly told me, 'He already broke the engagement 20 days ago.' I naturally protested, saying, 'Why did you not let me know 20 days back?' and she just smiled."

The protecting hand

For years, since terrorism started in the Punjab, there have been incidents every day in the province —some village, some town, railway lines tampered with, innocent people killed, banks looted at gun point, kidnapping, extortion and violence in some form or another. By the Master's protecting hand, the Dera carries on its activities in a normal manner.

Activities here remain the same, especially on monthly satsangs, when the attendance goes up to lakhs. Thousands of people also come and go every

Sunday. They are absolutely unconcerned about what is happening in the rest of the Punjab, such is their love and faith in the Master.

Maharaj Ji's first satsang

Though Maharaj Ji came to the Dera in October, 1951, he did not start giving satsang till much later. There were three elderly satsangis, Babu Gulab Singh, Sardar Gokal Singh and Baba Rameshwar Das, who used to hold satsang while Maharaj Ji sat on the dais giving darshan to the sangat.

Talking about how he started giving satsang, he said, "One day, I came to the Dera unannounced. The satsang had started when I reached. It was outside the library. I went and sat with the audience. A sevadar named Bhagat Ram was holding satsang on the shabd *Dil Ka Hujra*. I noticed that he was saying things which had no relevance to the shabd, nor did his exposition have any context with the teachings. He was only talking of miracles performed by the Great Master. I felt very uneasy and embarrassed.

"After the satsang, I asked Prof. Jagmohan Lal, who had come from Dalhousie with me, what he had to say about Bhagat Ram's satsang. Professor Sahib retorted, 'If you do not hold satsang, then what else should we expect?' I explained and pleaded with Professor Sahib that I knew nothing

MAHARAJ JI'S FIRST SATSANG

about Sant Mat teachings. I never attentively heard
Sardar Bahadur Ji's or Great Master's satsangs,
though I used to enjoy them. I never even noticed
which shabd was taken. I only knew one thing—
how to be steadfast on the three principles and how
to meditate.

"We had a lot of arguments, though I had great
respect for Professor Sahib. He was like a friend to
me, and I could take a lot of liberty with him. In
spite of our age difference, I could argue with him.
I had, in my college days, stayed with him in his
house at Kapurthala for a year. I stayed also with
his elder son at Rawalpindi for two years, when I
was graduating in Arts from Gordon College. He
emphatically argued with me and said, 'You are a
law graduate and were successful in your profession,
and right from childhood have been brought up in
this atmosphere. I cannot understand why it is not
possible for you to hold satsang.'

"Anyhow, in the evening, I was surprised
when Babu Gulab Singh came to me with one copy
each of *Sar Bachan* (poetry) and *Shabd Ki Mahima
Ke Shabd* in Punjabi, and told me that he had
selected fifteen shabds from each book for me
and I should discuss them with him, which would
help me to hold satsangs. I felt Professor Jagmohan
Lal's hand was behind this suggestion. I could
not say anything to Babu Gulab Singh, as he was
Babaji's satsangi, and I had great respect for
him. But he was shocked when I told him that
neither I knew Hindi nor I was fluent with Punjabi.
He just looked at my face blankly, and did not

know what to say. After some time I asked him if these books were available in Urdu. He told me he would check up and let me know, and left disappointed.

"After three days he again came with four volumes of the Adi Granth in Urdu, which I still have with me. He brought another small book of Soami Ji Maharaj's shabds printed in Urdu by Bakshi Maluk Chand. Ultimately, I started understanding from him the various aspects of the teachings. Meanwhile, Prof. Jagmohan Lal gave me a copy of *The Path of the Masters* to read, as it had to be reprinted, and he wanted some criticism of religions to be eliminated. It also helped me to understand the philosophy of Sant Mat.

"In winter I had gone to Sirsa for one and a half months. Munshi Ram Ji tried to teach me the Hindi alphabet as, he said, a lot of the teachings of saints were written in Hindi and it would be of great help to me to go through them. But he gave it up after a week, as I could not pick up more than a few letters.

"Anyhow, I held my first satsang and the shabd I took was from Tulsi Sahib, *Dil Ka Hujra*, and gradually I started giving satsang from shabds of Soami Ji Maharaj and the Adi Granth."

So, Maharaj Ji started to give satsang for two hours and sometimes even two and half hours, twice daily in those days. His inspiring soft voice and charismatic personality held the sangat spellbound. His lucid exposition—logical and convincing—was forceful. He often used to take two shabds, one from the Adi Granth and the other from Soami Ji Maharaj.

Maharaj Ji's father

Beji, when once talking to us about Maharaj Ji's father, told us that he was very particular about paying whatever he owed to anyone. He even paid for his own bier before he left the body. We became inquisitive and asked her to tell us the details.

She said that three or four days before his death, he called her and said, "I have given away everything to the children—only fifteen rupees remain with me. Give these ten rupees in seva," and then after keeping quiet for a moment, he continued, "and give these five rupees to Bhagat Singh, the carpenter." She did not understand why he had asked her to give money to the carpenter. When he passed away, the carpenter was called to make his bier, and then she and the other family members realized that he had made the payment in advance to the carpenter for the service to be rendered. Beji went on to say that he was a saintly person and was never attached to anything.

He was a unique example of a true disciple.

Start of initiation

Once Maharaj Ji, while talking about the time
he came to the 'gaddi' in October 1951, said,
"Though after some time I started holding satsang,
yet I did not start giving initiation after bhandaras
or monthly satsangs, which was the practice of
Sardar Bahadur Ji, Great Master and Babaji. However, there was great pressure on me from elder
satsangis in Dera to start initiation. I wanted to
delay as much as I could, and had decided that
when I did initiate, I would initiate only a few
and would not give general initiation to the masses.
It so happened that the very first initiation I gave
was to an American lady, Mrs. Kinzinger, under
compelling circumstances in April 1953. In June, the
same year, I initiated another three persons, all from
Mr. Khanna's family."

This reminded me of an interesting account
I had heard, and I wanted to obtain confirmation
from Maharaj Ji. I asked him, "Is it true that
when Sardar Bahadur Ji was ill and had stopped
initiating, Mr. Khanna had brought his mother,
wife and son to him for initiation? Sardar Bahadur
Ji had promised that when he would again start
initiating, Mr. Khanna's family would be among the
first. But Sardar Bahadur Ji passed away and you
kept the promise made by him." Maharaj Ji replied,
"Yes, it is true."

My husband, who was present at the 1953
October bhandara, told me that immediately after the
bhandara satsang, with tears flowing from his

eyes, Babu Gulab Singh, a highly respected satsangi of Babaji Maharaj, appealed to Maharaj Ji and pleaded that he start initiation and bestow on the seekers the gift of Nam, as the souls were thirsty and waiting. He added, "I humbly and respectfully implore you to open your treasure house and begin to bless seekers with initiation."

Everyone in the sangat was deeply touched by this speech, and tears filled every eye. They waited eagerly for Maharaj Ji to respond to the appeal of Babu Ji. Maharaj Ji said: "As Babu Ji has said, he and other elder satsangis have been urging me to start giving Nam. Huzur Sardar Bahadur Ji also left instructions to that effect. I am a slave of my Master and his sangat. . ." Then, his voice choked with emotion, Maharaj Ji paused for a few moments, tried to speak again but could not do so; tears were flowing from his eyes. He just got up and left.

The next day, 26th October 1953, Maharaj Ji started initiation. He was strict in selection, and out of over 700 presented to him, he selected only about 70. My husband was among these first fortunate few. He told me that in the evening Prof. Jagmohan Lal Ji came to them in the Guest House and said, "I have been instructed to take you to the initiation place tomorrow morning, so please be ready at about 7.30 a.m." My husband continued, "There were eight of us and we were all selected. During this initiation, Maharaj Ji kept standing, lightly reclining against the wall. He gave the impression that he was acting as a servant of his own beloved Satguru. But his face and eyes conveyed both love and power. He sat on the dais only at the time of imparting the sound." The pattern of strict selection continued for the next few initiations, but as Maharaj Ji started his satsang tours in India, gradually the number of seekers for initiation also increased.

Maharaj Ji said, "In spite of my resolve to initiate only a few, I was left with no choice. I had no heart to refuse the earnest seekers who were hungry for spirituality and keen to follow the path."

Thus opened the floodgates of grace and mercy, of which each Master is an embodiment. Everyone knows how the sangat has grown. Now Maharaj Ji initiates up to 20,000 people at a bhandara. Who can believe it? In 1987 the highest number of initiates in one year reached 112,114. Such was Maharaj Ji's selfless dedication to his Master, whose service he does lovingly, never giving thought to any kind of inconvenience or discomfort to himself.

Pertinent advice from Lala Munshi Ram

Maharaj Ji, in one of his reminiscent moods, said that he never got anything from the Dera seva store, even if it was available and he could pay for it. He always got it from the market. Explaining the reason for this, he said that in the beginning, when he had just come to the Dera, he wanted a bolt of

cloth for his turbans. He was sitting in the office
and asked Giani Karam Singh, who was in charge
of the store, to get one bolt from the market. Giani
Ji said, "Why do you want to buy from the market?
There are lots of bolts lying in the store, brought by
satsangis in seva. I will get one for you and you
may pay the market price for it." Maharaj Ji agreed
and told him to take the payment from him. He
then got up to come home. Lala Munshi Ram was
also sitting in the office and he asked Maharaj Ji if
he could accompany him, as he would like to talk
to him for a few minutes.

Whilst walking home with Maharaj Ji, Lala
Munshi Ram said, "Why do you want the cloth
from the store when you are paying for it? You
should always get it from the market. Many people
will see Giani Ji bring it from the store to you, but
no one will see you paying for it. These pieces of
cloth have come in seva. It could be misunderstood
by the sangat. Please make it a point never to get
anything from the store, but always obtain it from
the market." Maharaj Ji said, "From that day onwards, I have always purchased whatever I wanted
from the market and never got anything from the
Dera seva store. It was valuable advice that Rai
Sahib gave, and I very much appreciated it."

Continuing on the subject, Maharaj Ji told us
that once, a satsangi from Rajasthan brought a
beautifully shaped pitcher made of metal and
covered with woollen cloth, which is a speciality of
Rajasthan. It was made with his own hands and he
offered it to him saying that it would keep water

very cool during the summer months. "I have made it especially for you, please accept it." Maharaj Ji gently refused, saying that it would be of no use to him. So the satsangi offered it in seva and it was accepted.

At that time the then Secretary, Mr. Ahluwalia, was sitting in the office with Lala Munshi Ram. Mr. Ahluwalia said that the pitcher was very beautiful and it would be of no use in the Dera stores. He would like to use it and whatever was the cost, he would give the money in seva. In spite of Lala Munshi Ram's dissuading him, Mr. Ahluwalia took it and kept it on the window sill of his bedroom, which was above the office. The satsangi noticed it and after two or three days approached Maharaj Ji in the office. He said, "Maharaj Ji, I had made the pitcher especially for you and not for Mr. Ahluwalia. You did not accept it personally, but it was accepted in seva, then why is he using it?" Mr. Ahluwalia was also sitting in the office. He felt very embarrassed and returned the pitcher to the Dera stores. Lala Munshi Ram could not help saying to Mr. Ahluwalia, "Did I not tell you not to use anything which comes in seva to the Dera!"

Lifting of the ban on foreigners

In spite of all the terrorism rampant in the Punjab, in March 1989 the province was opened to foreigners. Satsangis from all parts of the world could now visit the Dera. This came about only by the grace of Maharaj Ji. Under his instructions, the Dera officials never ceased in their efforts to persuade the government to allow foreigners to visit the Dera. No effort was spared.

When the Home Minister, S. Buta Singh, came to Maharaj Ji at the Delhi Satsang Ghar to pay his respects, Maharaj Ji again pleaded the cause with him, saying, "It is heavy on my conscience that the foreign satsangis have to go through so much expense to be with me just for a week in Delhi and in Bombay." Maharaj Ji then took him to where the foreign visitors were having their dinner, to show how many had come for only a few days. The Home Minister was much impressed by the large gathering. When introducing him, Maharaj Ji told the foreigners that he had promised to help in getting the Punjab opened soon, so that satsangis from abroad could visit the Dera.

Then Maharaj Ji invited him to speak a few words to the guests. The Home Minister said, "I know Sant Mat and its teachings cannot be confined to the boundary of India alone. These teachings are universal and you should be allowed to go to the Dera to be with your Master. I will do my best to have the Punjab opened for all of you." Looking at the large gathering, he inquired about the number of visitors who had come. He was told they were about 800. He was amazed to know that they had come from twenty-five different countries and he was greatly impressed.

Pressure was also put on the Punjab Governor to move in the matter. Finally, in March, 1989, the ban was lifted. For the first time after five years, foreign satsangis could visit the Punjab. Many who were attending the Delhi satsang were granted permission by Maharaj Ji to come to the Dera. They were overjoyed.

A few weeks later the Governor of the Punjab, Mr. S.S. Ray, came to the Dera and was astonished to see such a large gathering of visitors from so many different countries. He had tea with them and was happy to mix with them. Although the situation in the Punjab was still the same, the foreign satsangis did not hesitate to come; such was the faith they had in their Master and such was their longing for his darshan which brought them here, irrespective of alarming conditions prevailing in the Punjab.

Due to Maharaj Ji's compassion and kindheartedness and his care and concern for his disciples, he allowed them, during the years when the Punjab was closed to foreigners, to attend satsangs held by him in Delhi thrice a year and also in Bombay once a year. He asked the Delhi and Bombay managements to provide all possible facilities to satsangis coming from abroad, to look after their comfort and give them all the help they needed. He gave instructions for all meals to be served to them free of charge. In the Delhi Satsang Ghar all available accommodation was offered for their stay. The sevadars served them with love and concern, and all who came were deeply touched by their devoted service. They went back, hearts filled with love and eyes full of tears, grateful for the kindness, consideration and loving hospitality of the beloved Master.

Maharaj Ji, in spite of his busy satsang activities, held daily English meetings, and met all of them in groups from different countries. He also gave individual interviews to whomsoever needed it. His concern for them was that of a loving father; his kindness, boundless.

Thus, in September 1989, the Guest House at the Dera opened on a regular basis for Westerners, and permission was granted by Maharaj Ji to Western satsangis to visit the Dera for a maximum stay of 30 days. On learning this, satsangis were filled with joy and gratitude. There were some who had never seen their Master and others who had never been to the Dera. They were thrilled to be here. It was a continuous flow. The highest number in one day went up to 449 in February 1990. In view of the large attendance of foreign guests this year, Maharaj Ji started the construction of two additional blocks in the International Guest House compound, one for ladies and the other for men, with a capacity to accommodate 306 more guests. He also decided to extend the dining hall and the coffee house in order to serve 500 guests at a time. In all, from September to April (except from January 8 to February 10 when the Guest House closes), 1,863 foreign guests visited the Dera.

During this time guests came from all over the world, representing forty different countries. Among them were some doctors and nurses who

offered their services to the Beas Charitable Hospital. Many guests undertook seva in the Guest House
and did it with great love and dedication. The whole
atmosphere in the Guest House was one of a large
happy family. With terrorism, cruelty and turmoil rife
in the world, here in the heart of the Punjab, the
Dera was an oasis of peace and joy, nurtured by our
loving and compassionate Master.

<hr />

Rao Sahib

Maharaj Ji once narrated an incident illustrating
Rao Sahib's devotion and simplicity of heart.
During one summer month in the fifties, Maharaj Ji
had just reached Dalhousie with his wife, to be
with his children who were studying there. The same
day a telegram came from Rao Sahib announ-
cing that he was reaching Dalhousie. Maharaj Ji
and his wife were naturally worried, and thought
that there must be something urgent or serious,
which had forced Rao Sahib to come all of a
sudden.

On his arrival, Rao Sahib, who looked quite
perturbed, wanted to talk to Maharaj Ji immediately.
Declining even to take a cup of tea, he said, "First
I must talk to you."

Maharaj Ji took Rao Sahib aside, who told him
with tears flowing from his eyes, "Maharaj Ji, I am
not your father-in-law. I am just one of your disciples, your servant."

Maharaj Ji said, "Rao Sahib, please compose yourself. Tell me what has happened." Between sobs and tears, Rao Sahib said, "Purshottam Das, a satsangi who gives satsang in Delhi, read out a couplet which means that disciples of a saint, from all corners of the world, benefit and are emancipated, but his in-laws, his paternal and maternal relations, and his close childhood friends remain devoid of his grace. On hearing this, I felt extremely distressed. I could not sleep the whole night. After you were appointed the Master at Dera, I have always looked upon you as the Satguru, never as a son-in-law. I am not your father-in-law. I am only your disciple."

Maharaj Ji, deeply moved by Rao Sahib's innocence and devotion, lovingly answered, "Rao Sahib, you are a disciple of the Great Master. How can your being my father-in-law change your relationship with the Great Master? I am honoured to be your son-in-law."

Maharaj Ji then explained to Rao Sahib that this couplet only meant that close relations and friends of a saint sometimes look upon him as a son, a brother, a son-in-law, a husband, a father or a friend, and fail to recognize his spiritual greatness. They take him as an ordinary human being. Therefore, due to that attitude, they fail to benefit from the saint because of their close association. Maharaj Ji added, "Rao Sahib, you are a loving and devoted disciple of the Great Master. You should not worry."

Hearing Maharaj Ji's words, Rao Sahib felt greatly relieved and happy.

Disturbances in the Punjab

Once, referring to the disturbances in the Punjab, Maharaj Ji said in satsang: "This land of Punjab, which has been called the land of the Gurus, is sacred to us. From here the Gurus gave their message of love and devotion. This land has been blessed by the divine touch of the Gurus' lotus feet. Men and women come from distant places to apply the dust of this land to their foreheads, to kiss it, because the feet of these great saints have trodden on this land. Today, if brothers spill the blood of brothers on this hallowed land, what could be more painful, more disgraceful?

"This is because today we have forgotten the teachings of the Gurus. We have become slaves to ritualism. We are the devotees of temples, mosques and gurdwaras. We are no more the devotees of the one Lord. The true devotees of the Lord not only love Him, but also love all His creation. This is the message of all saints, this is the message of Guru Nanak and his great successors— a message of love, of universal brotherhood. Deeply steeped in their love for God, they loved all humanity. They taught us to love the Lord, to love one another.

"Guru Amar Das says, 'Lord, every being, every creature, belongs to you, and you belong to everyone. Whom can I call bad or inferior, when there is none other but you?"

(Adi Granth, M.3, p.425)

———

Indo-Pak War – 1965

In reference to the 1965 war Maharaj Ji told us, "In September 1965, I was in Dalhousie along with my family members and Mr. and Mrs. Kundan Sondhi. One day Kundan came to me, right after lunch, and said, 'I have just heard on the BBC News that a war between India and Pakistan has broken out.' I said to him, 'Let us go at once to the Dera.' When we were driving through Pathankot, we heard the sound of bombing somewhere around that area, but we drove on to the Dera. There was quite a movement of army vehicles on the road, but we managed somehow to reach the Dera safely by that evening.

"At night we heard a lot of bombardment near the Dera, and in the morning we came to know that Pakistan was trying to destroy the Beas rail and road bridge. The next day more than half of the population of Amritsar migrated, and people rushed to Jullundur, which is south of Amritsar. But to my surprise I found many buses and trucks of satsangis coming to the Dera for satsang. I asked them, 'Aren't you frightened of the bombardment?' There was no sign of any kind of fear on their faces. Everybody thought that no place could be more safe than this one. No resident of the Dera left the colony. They seemed to be happy all through, and all our activities remained the same.

"At that time we were building the main block of the International Guest House, and there was a shortage of cement. One cement stockist from Amritsar, who was fleeing to Jullundur, stopped here on his way and approached me. Only the week before we were requesting him for 100 bags, which he refused to sell to us. Now he said, 'I have about 4,000 bags of cement in my store. Please go there, collect that cement from Amritsar and I'll collect the money later on.' By Maharaj Ji's grace, our whole Guest House was completed, and he came after about a month to collect the payment for the cement."

***

"I was in the colony all through the conflict. One night an army officer, along with Mr. Khanna, our then Secretary, came to me at ten o'clock at night and told me that they had news that the army ammunition depot, which is adjacent to our colony, may be bombarded, and may affect us. The officer said, 'You'd better dig trenches, and we will sound the siren for the occasion, so your residents can go to the trenches at that time.' I told him, 'There is hardly anybody here under the age of 60. Half of them will break their legs while running to the trenches, and some of them may even faint if this

news goes to them, so we'd better not do anything.
We'll just take a chance.' I asked him how many
anti-aircraft guns the army had around the colony. At
first he hesitated, then he said, 'Sir, you are our
only anti-aircraft gun.' By Maharaj Ji's grace there
was no incident at the Dera nor near about, and
everything passed off quite peacefully. After a couple
of days, a lot of anti-aircraft guns were fitted around
the ammunition depot.

"Louise, who was also here, commented on how
much unnecessary suffering is caused by war. I
replied to her that if politicians were made to fight,
then they would realize it. They just sit in air-
conditioned rooms and order the soldiers to fight.
If they were sent to the front, only then they
would know what war is. The modern wars are
worse than ever before; even the civilians are as
much exposed to danger as military people, may-
be more, because poor innocent people are not
even equipped to defend themselves. If, at twelve in
the night, a bomb falls, hundreds of lives are lost
for nothing."

Maharaj Ji's reminiscences

"Beji, my mother, who is about 92, has a
remarkable memory. She often talks about the Great
Master and the Dera during the early days.

"When Beji first came to the Dera, which was
soon after her marriage, the Dera was still a

wilderness, and there were only a few buildings. The Great Master used to stay in one of the five rooms on the upper floor of the building[1] situated to the east of the Great Master's house. Babaji's room was there, but it was still a small hut with a thatched verandah in the front. The two rooms where Bibi Rali lived were also there, but were part of the langar; only the inner portion of the langar had been built at that time. The maximum number of sangat served in the langar used to be about 150 on Sundays.

"Whenever Beji and other members of the family came to the Dera, they stayed in the rooms on the ground floor of the building referred to earlier.

"The Great Master, in all humility, used to draw the first pitcher of water from the well and bring it to the langar. He also used to bake the first chapati on the iron plate after Bibi Rukko had rolled it. It was only after this that the sangat drew more water from the well and other ladies joined in rolling and baking chapatis.

"The Great Master had his own separate kitchen. He never partook of food in the langar. There were no bathrooms, and the Great Master used to take his bath at the well. Later, he got a bathroom built for himself. In earlier days, he even used to sleep on the floor. But after some

---

1. This building with 4 rooms on the ground floor and 5 on the upper, was built during Babaji's lifetime in 1902. Babaji had also stayed in the first room situated in the east on the upper floor.

time, on the insistence of satsangis, he started using
a bed."

***

"After Babaji left the world, the Great Master
was still in service and used to visit the Dera during his holidays to hold satsang.

"Bibi Rukko was a dominant person, virtually
looking after the Dera administration. She was
very stern with the satsangis, and always wanted
them to dress simply, especially the ladies, when
they came to the Dera to attend satsang. She never
hesitated even to use a rod in anger, if she felt the
need.

"Towards the end of her life, she went to stay
with a few devoted satsangis in a village near
Amritsar. After some time the Great Master brought
her back to Dera, but after about a year she again
went to the same village.

"Near the end of her life, she told the satsangis
with whom she was staying that the Great Master
had come within and had asked her to accompany
him. She refused to go with him, saying, 'I'll not
go with you. Babaji must come and take me.' The
next day she told the people that Babaji had
appeared and told her, 'I have instructed Babu
Sawan Singh to take you back home.' She smiled
and told Babaji, 'I am ready to go with him.' Soon
after that she died."

The value of seva

Once, a satsangi lady told Maharaj Ji that as she had no income of her own, she always asked her husband to give her some money for offering in seva. "Will this seva be of any benefit to me? Does it have any value?"

Maharaj Ji replied, "Yes, if both of you are happy in giving this seva." Maharaj Ji further explained this by giving the example of a satsangi with one leg who used to come during the bhandaras. "He used to come from the hills of Himachal, and was very poor. Just to save money to give in seva, he used to walk from his village in the hills to the Dera, with the help of his crutches, covering a distance of over 75 miles. Once he was brought to me during 'money seva' by Mr. Bolakani. He offered one rupee in seva. Looking to his poverty, I asked the sevadars not to accept it, but he burst into tears, and I had to accept his offering.

"How can you value this seva? Is it not worth much more than the hundreds and thousands that the rich give? The value of seva is not in *how much* one offers, but in the feelings and love with which it is offered."

***

I am reminded of another occasion when Maharaj Ji expressed himself on this point. It was when the sangat was engaged in the seva of filling one of the large and deep ravines. A senior

satsangi from South Africa was sitting near Maharaj
Ji. Observing some ladies carrying only a handful of
earth in their baskets, he remarked, "What is the use
of their seva? They are carrying so little."

Maharaj Ji replied, "It is not how much a person carries that is important. It is the love with
which one carries it that counts. They are doing
it purely out of love."

***

Once Maharaj Ji mentioned that when the
Satsang Ghar in the Dera was being constructed,
S. Narain Singh, a very rich and well-known
contractor of Delhi and a devoted satsangi, requested the Great Master that he might be given the seva
of building the whole Satsang Ghar. The Great
Master replied, "No, I want every satsangi, even
the poorest of the poor, to be given an opportunity
to offer something in seva, even if it is only a
rupee or half a rupee. I would also like every
satsangi, rich and poor, young and old, to participate
in the construction, even if they carry only a
handful of sand or a few bricks. Their smallest
effort is precious to me, every drop of perspiration
shed by them is valuable. This is seva of love and
devotion."

How much the sangat has achieved through
sharing in this loving seva for their Master can be
seen in every corner of the Dera today.

Excerpts from Maharaj Ji's letters to friends

August 10th, 1963

Since you are there, I think now you should try to make best use of the situation. There is nothing which a man cannot do with the love and support of a wife. He seems to lean too much on you, so you should give him the required strength. I am sure, with your love and his soft and gentle qualities, he will be able to adjust to the situation.

***

August 20th, 1965

Radha Soami!

I know a storm must be brewing within you on my such an unusual and uncalled-for long silence. Well, I plead guilty. What should I write you? Much water has flowed under the bridge. What is the use of writing, which makes no sense with you, as you received all news concerning me through so many sources, and I cannot write what I want to? Perhaps silence is the language of the heart.

***

September 17th, 1965

I am guilty of keeping silence for all these months. I do not know what is wrong with me. I just cannot write to my near and dear ones. I am always with them, but just cannot keep contact through writing. Ever since you and . . . have left, I am on the move, and I know I owe you a lot of explanation for not reaching Delhi before your departure; but I always feel explanation is only a lack of faith in the other person.

You know what is happening on our border. We are under constant air raids. By Maharaj Ji's grace we are all safe here in this little colony, and I have faith nothing will happen here. I have been advised to leave by my lovers, but I find no better fort than this. I know anything can happen on the border, but His protecting hand is always on me and His sangat.

***

June 9th, 1968

Radha Soami!

After shaking me, you have gone to deep sleep again. By Maharaj Ji's grace, my whole trip is just wonderful and pleasant. Oh! people are just loving and kind everywhere I go, and do everything to make my stay a pleasant one. I do not remember having done anything in this life to deserve so much love and regards. In spite of all that I am, Maharaj Ji is too good to me. I am so happy and so well fed that I have put on five pounds of weight.

***

January 20th, 1964

Radha Soami!

Rao Sahib died on the 13th early morning, in Sen's Nursing Home (New Delhi) and his body was brought to the Dera the same evening, though the cremation took place the next morning. I was informed at Calcutta during the early hours of the morning and managed to get the morning flight to Delhi and reach Beas the same evening, rather, along with the other party carrying Rao Sahib's body to Beas. His Bhog ceremony will also be performed here at the Dera on the 25th. As you all know, he was a grand old soul, humble, simple in nature and sincere in his approach. He was very devoted to the Great Master. He was very popular amongst satsangis and commanded a lot of respect. I was fortunate to have him as my father-in-law; I had great respect and love for him.

You must have read in the newspapers about the disturbances in Calcutta. Incidentally, I was there during those days on my satsang tour. I was holding satsang at Mohammedan Park, predominated mostly by Muslims, and had one of the most unique experiences of my life on this satsang tour.

While I was holding satsang, shooting, arson, and firing were going on within our sight. Though there was a gathering of about three thousand people, not a single one moved or felt concerned as to what was happening all around. I was myself surprised to witness such faith and love. The satsang went on for a couple of hours, and just after the satsang dispersed, the military took over and put a curfew there. Every satsangi returned home quite safely. None of us were hurt at all.

***

Mrs. Bharat Ram, who was with Maharaj Ji in Calcutta on this satsang tour, told me that while going to the satsang, Maharaj Ji was sitting in the car with two local satsangis and the secretary of the Calcutta Satsang, and she was following them in another car. Suddenly her car stopped; Maharaj Ji, noticing it, stopped his car, and asked her to sit in his car. Soon after, when his car started to move, it was hit by a bullet, but Maharaj Ji told the driver to drive on, and they all reached the satsang pandal safely.

Mrs. Bharat Ram told us that after the satsang, when Maharaj Ji reached home, he was informed by the secretary that the whole pandal had been burnt. The initiation, scheduled for the next day, was therefore held in Mrs. Bharat Ram's house instead of the pandal.

She also told us that when they were leaving Delhi for Calcutta, she was with Maharaj Ji when he visited his father-in-law in Sen's Nursing Home. In the car she asked Maharaj Ji if Rao Sahib would become all right. Maharaj Ji replied, "He will be no more when we return, and I have already told Khanna Sahib (then secretary of the Dera) to make all arrangements." So when the news came of his

death, despite the curfew, Maharaj Ji got a seat on
the plane to Delhi.

———

Letters from Lala Munshi Ram

While looking into the Dera records, I came
across some interesting confidential letters written
by Lala Munshi Ram to Maharaj Ji during Sardar
Bahadur Ji's lifetime. In one of the letters dated
6-6-51, he wrote that Sardar Bahadur Ji had asked
Lala Munshi Ram to purchase savings deposits of
Rs. 50,000/- from the Dera account in the joint
names of Sardar Bahadur Ji and Maharaj Ji, and he
wanted Maharaj Ji's signature on the second form.

The second letter was dated 22-6-51, in which
Lala Munshi Ram wanted Maharaj Ji's signatures
on four application forms. In the third letter dated
22-9-51, he wrote to Maharaj Ji that Sardar Bahadur
Ji wanted to open an account in the joint names of
himself and Maharaj Ji.[1] Photo-copies of the original
letters are attached.[2]

The last letter was written just a month before
Sardar Bahadur Ji's passing away. Sardar Bahadur Ji
had already decided who would be the next
Master, but did not disclose it to Maharaj Ji during
his lifetime, for reasons best known to him.

———

1. At that time all Dera property—movable and immovable—was
legally in the name of Sardar Bahadur Ji as the immediate successor
to the Great Master.

2. This has been referred to earlier under "A veiled hint" on p.10
of this book.

The lamp was ready to be kindled. All it needed was the tender and brief touch of a flame to enable it to shine in its hitherto concealed effulgence.

***

Dera, Beas: 6-6-51

Dear S. Charan Singh ji:

Sardar Bahadurji has directed me to deposit Rs. 50000/- of Dera Fund in Ten-Year Treasury Savings Deposits in the joint names of himself and your good self; interest and principle to be payable to either or survivor (for precautions' sake). Therefore I am enclosing a printed form for your signatures at the place marked X. Please also let me know if you hold any Treasury Savings Deposits in order to enable me to fill the appropriate column in the form. Please keep the matter entirely secret and reply soon.

With loving regards

Yours Affectionately,

Munshi Ram
Secretary.

***

Dera Baba Jaimal Singh
Beas, 22-6-51

Dear Charan Singh ji:

I am enclosing herewith four application forms for your signatures at the place marked X. Shri Sardar Bahadur Sahib intends to purchase five certificates of Rs. ten thousand each for facility of encashment.

I hope you must have returned from the marriage. My sincere congratulations. My Radha Soami to yourself and S. Harbans Singh ji. Please keep this matter confidential.

With kind regards

Yours Affectionately,

Munshi Ram
Secretary

***

Dera Baba Jaimal Singh
Beas—22.9.51

Dear S. Charan Singh ji:

As Shri Hazur Sardar Bahadur Sahib wishes to open some accounts in your joint name please put your signatures on the enclosed forms at all the places marked X and return them to me at an early date under registered postal cover.

All is well at the Dera. Daya Mehar from Hazur. S. Bachint Singh has returned from Dalhousie.

Yours Affectionately,

Munshi Ram
Secretary.

———

Dera Dun: 6-6-51

Dear S. Charan Singh ji:

Sardar Bahadur ji has directed me to deposit Rs. 5000/ of Dera Fund in Ten-Year Treasury savings Deposits in the joins names of himself and your good self; interest and principal to be payable to either or survivor (for precaution' sake). Therefore I am enclosing a printed form for your signatures, at the place marked X. Please also let me know if you hold any Treasury savings Deposits in order to enable me to fill the appropriate columns in the form. Please keep the matter entirely secret and reply soon.

With loving regards

Yours Affectionately,
Munshi Ram
Secretary.

Dear Baba Jaimini singh

Bess. 22 - 6 - 51,

Dear Charan singh ji :

I am enclosing herewith four
application form for your signature
at the place marked X. shri
sardar Bahadur sahib
intends to purchase five certificates of Rs. ten thousand each for
facility of encashment.

I hope you must have returned
from the marriage. My sincere
congratulations. My Radha.

swami to yourself and s.

Hardass Sitji ji. Please

keep this matter confidential

with kind regards

Yours Affectionately

Munyoti Ram

secretary

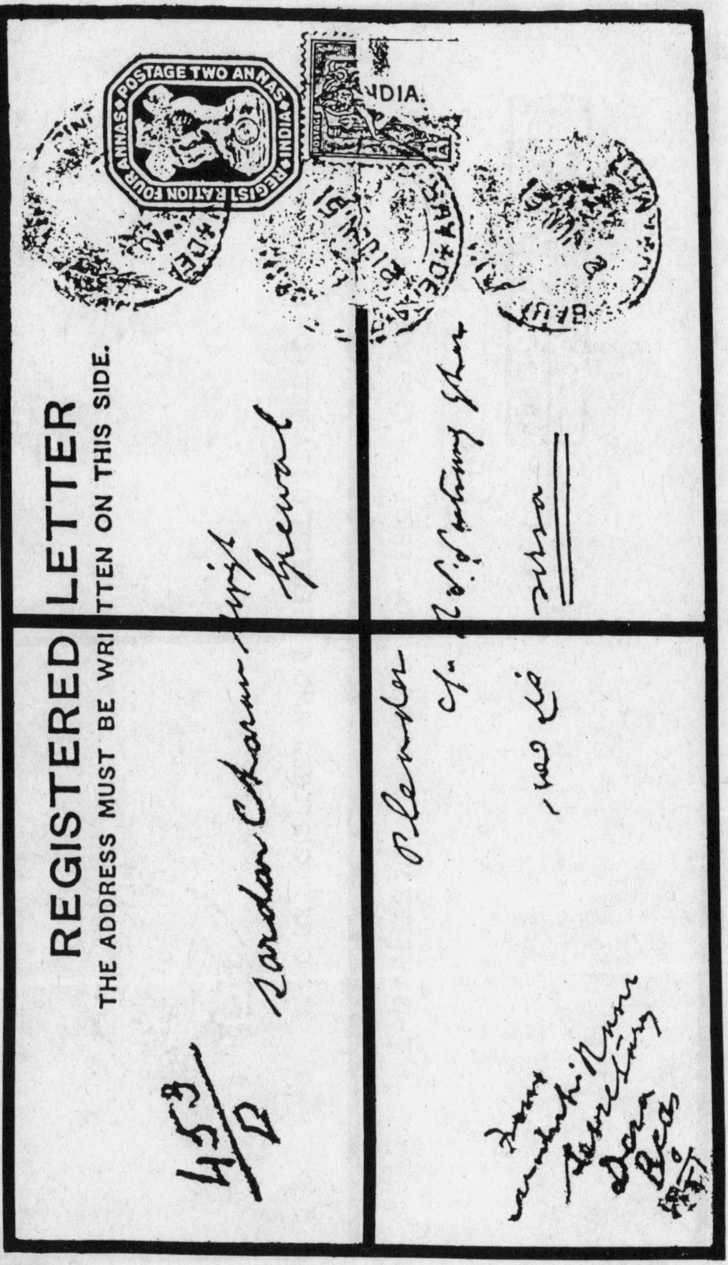
REGISTERED LETTER
THE ADDRESS MUST BE WRITTEN ON THIS SIDE.
POSTAGE TWO ANNAS
REGISTRATION FOUR ANNAS
INDIA

R 453

DERA BABA JAIMAL SINGH
BRANCH OFFICE
AMRITSAR DISTRICT

THIS LETTER MUST BE GIVEN TO AN OFFICER OF THE POST OFFICE

TO BE REGISTERED AND A RECEIPT OBTAINED FOR IT.

REG.
25 JUN 5

Dera Baba Jaimal Singh

Beas – 22.9.51

Dear S. Charan Singh ji:

As s/d Hzur Sardar Bahadur Sahib wishes to open some accounts in your joint name please put your signatures on the enclosed forms at all the places marked X and return them to me at an early date under registered postal cover.

All; well at the Dera. Durga meher for Hzur. S. Bachint Syt has returned from Dalhousie.

Yours Affectionately

Munshi Ram

secretary.

Excerpts from Maharaj Ji's letters

Los Angeles, Calif., U.S.A.
May 15th, 1964

Miss Hilger and Sondhi have also been kept too busy to write. However, I may add that I am very happy to see the American devotees of Huzur Maharaj Ji in their own country. The moment I arrived at the airport, there was a scene worth beholding, and it can hardly be described in words. Tears were rolling from their eyes, their throats were choked with emotion, their lips were fluttering with love, and their hearts were dancing with joy. They are really very fine satsangis. I am glad I could make up to see them in their homeland.

                          ***

Niagara Falls
Canadian Side
June 21st, 1964

Tomorrow I'll be back to New York and will get my boat on the 24th to London. I am looking forward very anxiously to being on the boat, so that I may get some time to sleep, relax and rest before I start my hectic activities of satsang again from London onwards.

My whole trip has been a great experience to me, and it is really a wonderful privilege and delight to see Huzur Maharaj Ji's devotees, thousands of miles away from the Dera, following his teachings in such surroundings, which are the least congenial to satsang atmosphere. But I have no words to describe their love, devotion and affection, and their acceptance to learn and to practise the teachings and to get rid of this world of illusion. No doubt they have kept me very busy, but by His grace my health took everything quite normally, and I always felt within me a genuine happiness and joy to attend to all such hectic activities of satsang. By His grace my whole trip has been quite successful.

***

Johannesburg
South Africa
21st May, 1966

Radha Soami.

I am sorry to know from your letter that your father has died and you are now in England for his last ceremonies. I know what you feel, as a few years ago I myself passed through the same experience. It is a great blessing to have the elders guiding us and looking after our interest in life. Anyhow, this is the way of the world, and everybody has to leave everyone. May Maharaj Ji give you strength to face this catastrophe, and may the Lord give peace to the departed soul!

***

November 4th, 1966

I am sorry to note from your letter that you feel emotionally quite disturbed. No doubt you are quite mature, but still there are many things which one learns as one grows. You are passing through a time when you are likely to be attracted by passing fancies and deceptive emotions, so you have to fight with them to know their reality as to where you stand. You need constant guidance through this age (18 years), perhaps more guidance now than before. So do not hesitate to consult with and confide in your parents.

***

November 13th, 1966

No doubt my tour in the Himalayas was very tiring, but it is really a unique experience to see simple hill people, coming from such great distances to attend satsang. Sant Mat is spreading like wildfire in the hills. The people are very honest, innocent and sincere, and they easily grasp these simple teachings. Our so-called civilization has not much penetrated into the hills yet, so the people are quite straightforward and honest. It is a sight to see the rolling tears at the time of hearing satsang and their eyes full with love and affection. Yet they do not say a word to express what they feel.

I often wonder how Maharaj Ji could reach those places, especially in those days when there were hardly any roads. I am told he often walked for ten to twenty miles, and sometimes rode a horse all day just to reach those spots and stay in those small huts, which are not even well ventilated, what to say of having an attached bathroom. His efforts are bearing fruit now, as Sant Mat is spreading far and wide in the Himachal area. We have so many beautiful satsang ghars at various places, constructed by Maharaj Ji, and quite comfortable for me and the sangat to stay in them.

***

Auckland
June 24th, 1968

In any way it must be a strange experience to stay all alone—far away from the madding crowd. Actually such an opportunity is God-sent, as we realize deep within ourselves as to where we stand in relation to this world. The Lord has His own ways and means to pull us towards Him. I am glad you are attending to your meditation.

***

You know that all our life is, in fact, the adjustment of our karmic account. It is difficult to say what is for our good. Better it is to leave everything in the hands of the Lord, and to be happy at what he does.

Please do not feel perturbed at all. Turn to bhajan and simran, and you will be happy by

abiding in the will of the Lord. View all your surroundings and relations as if this world was meant
for adjustment of our accounts with them. Thank the
Lord for what He has bestowed upon you, and keep
your mind in bhajan and simran.

***

Washington
May 21st, 1970

By Maharaj Ji's grace my tour is just wonderful from a satsang point of view. I am collecting a
lot of audience everywhere I go, as you know from
Janak's letters to Mr. Khanna. People are hungry for
spirituality, and they realize now that material
achievements have not led them to any happiness or
peace of mind, and strange enough, they are not
very rigid in their Christian beliefs. They have
started thinking openly, are trying to come out from
the traditional beliefs, and it is very easy to reach
them through the Bible.

My health is fairly good, though these long
flights are terrible, and then the change of time
zones gives one many sleepless nights. But I am
very happy in the discharge of my duty and in
finding people full of love and devotion and so
receptive to Maharaj Ji's teachings. No doubt,
sometimes it is very tiring to go through the same
routine every day, but then it gives one a strange
consolation and happiness when one feels that
Maharaj Ji's mission is being fulfilled by His grace.

Janak is very helpful and gives beautiful lectures on Sant Mat. His approach is intellectual, philosophical and clear, and people are quite impressed. Otherwise also, he is a very good companion. It is interesting and amusing to watch him always being lost in himself, especially when he passes through customs and immigration.

***

I understand your emotions and appreciate your one-pointed love for your Master. But you have certain commitments and obligations towards others and your family members. You must try to fulfil them with love and sincerity. Love for the Master does not mean that one is free to neglect the family members. Love should make you more understanding, more tolerant. It should make you a better wife, a better mother, a better person in all respects.

Love does not mean that we should ignore our duties, that we should turn our back upon worldly responsibilities. Love should make you an ideal person in life, a shining example for others to follow. Seeing you, they in turn are likely to be attracted towards the path of Sant Mat. So, try to fulfil your obligations towards your family members with a feeling that the Master is always with you, is helping you. Love the Master, but give them what is due to them.

***

Minnesota
U.S.A.
June 8th, 1970

My routine at every center is the same. I start interviews in the morning and then have a coffee-break meeting with a small number of local satsangis. Sometimes this carries me to 11.30 a.m. or so. Then I have to attend lunch at somebody's house. Since the distances here are great, it takes 45 minutes or an hour to drive there, one hour for lunch and I am back at the hotel by 3.00 or 3.30 p.m. Anyway, I don't remember having slept before 11.00 p.m. since I left India, but I feel fine and I am keeping good health. I have no complaints.

All the people are loving and devoted. They want to do everything for me. Also satsangis follow me from one center to another, and most of the plane is usually full of them. The hotels, where I stay, are crowded with seekers and initiates. I think I am giving good business to the airlines, the hotels and the photographers, without getting any commission from them!

One thing which I especially like about the Americans is that they are quite honest, frank and sincere—sometimes too frank. You always know where you stand with them. If they love you, they never hesitate to tell you and express it, but if they hate you, it is clearly written on their face. There is great harmony among the satsangis this time and they are cooperating and adjusting to one another's viewpoint. I fear that they have become somewhat

self-centered, perhaps because of modern conven-
iences and the effect of television. Individually
everyone is gold, but collectively I don't know what
happens to them. At least I have no problem with
the satsang centers, because I find much love
amongst them.

You will be glad to know that at Detroit I met
all of the elder and seasoned satsangis in connection
with forming a central organization for America. It
made me very happy that they all came to an agree-
ment that all other trusts and organizations should
be dissolved into this one central organization. What
pleases me the most is the love and understanding
among them. They see that there should be one
central organization to control and help the satsang
affairs of all America.

***

February 2nd, 1972

I think this heart attack was due to too much
stress and strain I had to go through for the last
couple of years. Perhaps my heart found it difficult
to cooperate with my increasing satsang activities. I
got it on 26th November and was immediately
admitted in Medical Institute at Delhi, but couldn't
get the complete treatment as the war broke out
and I had to rush to the Dera on 6th December.
Since then I am practically on rest, which has done
me a lot of good. Now the doctor has given me
clearance, even to resume my normal activities.

***

Please do not run to any spiritualist to get me healed, as I am not in their hands at all. There is someone else who is looking after us, and why show your lack of faith in Him? It looks very odd to me, to know about this way of thinking of yours, especially when I have condemned spiritual healing quite boldly in my books. You should have faith in Maharaj Ji. Whatever he does is always for our best. We have to play the role assigned to us, as long as he wants us to play it. Not a minute or second can be added to it by any spiritual healer, nor by any doctor. Please assure me that you won't do any such thing, as, besides embarrassing me, it also leaves a very bad taste in my mouth.

***

The Great Master's blessing and protecting hand is always on his sheep, even the stray ones. I am sorry to say that slowly, slowly you are drifting away from satsang and thus denying your children the holy atmosphere of the Dera and the sobering influence of satsang. Your visit to the Dera is hardly worth the name, ·and that too was not for satsang purposes. You are not even in touch with the Dera publications.

***

January 29th, 1976

Ever since I have come from my Bombay tour, I have been very busy, rather on my toes, attending to satsang activities. The Guest House has remained filled with foreigners, and they keep me quite occupied. I have just come from a long satsang tour of Nagpur, Calcutta and Madras. I again leave for Delhi tomorrow to hold satsang and then to Gwalior, after which I make a dash for a day to Indore, to attend some marriage, and thus reach Sirsa on 7th, again to leave for Indore on satsang tour on 13th. Anyway, I'll be at Beas from 22nd February until 5th March.

People's devotion and kindness don't let me sleep and live in peace, and I am always moving from place to place just to visit them. I know how both of you feel concerned about my health and especially about my operation, but I hardly have any time to think about myself. The trouble is not so acute as requiring my coming to England for the operation. Everything is in the hands of Maharaj Ji and I am happy to go through his planning.

***

October 5th, 1983

No doubt, I have been running about on satsang tours, but still that is no reason that I have no time to attend to my personal correspondence. We are so occupied with this Punjab problem, that we hardly get into a mood to write to anyone. There seems to be no end and solution to this, nor have the politicians any interest in any solution. They are more concerned with their 'chairs'. Let us hope for the best. Anyway, by His grace we are all safe and the Dera is absolutely peaceful. Except for the newspapers, we hardly know what is happening around us.

You will be sorry to know that Bhua Ji[1] left her body on 27th, at about 1.45 a.m. The end was quite peaceful, and she was quite conscious till her last evening. I met her at about 6 o'clock on the 26th evening, and she gave me a smile and a look of recognition. Anyway, we were expecting the end. In fact, I was personally anxious for the end to come—since it was to come—it was unnecessary to prolong her misery, to keep her tied down in that frail body. She was an institution by herself. She came to the Dera at the age of seven, staying until she reached ninety-two. I don't recollect her going out of the Dera except on a tour with me to Bombay and Indore, and occasionally to Sirsa with me. You know what she meant to all of us, but still we have to accept His will.

Committee meeting
advice from Maharaj Ji

It's all right if you disagree inside the committee, so long as you argue objectively and without personal criticism. But then all of you must make a single decision and speak with one voice outside of the committee meeting. No one outside the meeting should hear of inside disagreements. These are the basic principles of democracy.

---

1. Bibi Rali.

Why should there be disharmony? Satsangis
are all brothers and sisters. We all have the same
Father. Your object should be to please the sangat.
You are rendering service, not wielding authority.
This committee should not be about showing off or
bossing people. It's about serving the sangat, not
dictating. The human mind may trick us into believ-
ing we're important. We're not. We're just here to
please the sangat.

———

Excerpts from Col. Berg's introduction
at the Unitarian Society, Minneapolis
May 28, 1964

Sant Mat, as the teachings are called, goes
strictly along the line of the top-ranking saints of
Persia, India and China, and the Sant Mat centers
are not composed of the usual type of orders of
sadhus and fakirs that we see in India. The initiates
do not abandon the world, but lead a normal family life and carry out their spiritual practice while
discharging their worldly duties. The centers emphasize that one who cannot face the trials and tribulations of worldly life, would hardly be fit to travel
the more difficult spiritual path.

The Masters themselves are examples in this,
and have earned their living as weavers, potters,
shoemakers, goldsmiths, farmers, engineers and in
various other professions. The present Master,
Charan Singh Ji Maharaj, is a lawyer and farmer.

One of the characteristics of the Beas mystics is that normally they do not interfere with the destiny of their initiates. They insist on the disciples' submitting themselves to the will of God—a submission which they hold is an essential spiritual discipline. They do not offer to give success in business, examinations or law court cases, nor to secure employment for the unemployed. They emphasize that one must face happiness and misery, success and failure, days of joy and days of sorrow, with equanimity, and carry out one's spiritual practice in the midst of changing circumstances. If one is too elated with wealth and prosperity to practise spiritual exercises, or too depressed to practise them owing to failures, trials and tribulations, when is one going to do them? The Masters here insist on the initiates facing life as it comes and carrying out their spiritual task in the midst of worldly life. They also insist upon them going about like normal human beings, with no outward sign whatsoever to distinguish them from others. There are no ochre-colored clothes here nor any 'habits' or uniforms.

Excerpts from Maharaj Ji's address in Minneapolis May 28, 1964

I have been greatly impressed by what I have seen and heard of the scientific achievements and material well-being realized in this country, but I have felt that the people, nevertheless, are aware of the fact that these attainments have not brought them true happiness. This is probably true, and if we analyse the situation with an unbiased mind, we will find that the real peace and happiness we are seeking have remained a distant dream because our pursuits have been through political, social and economic means. We have never tried to explore possibilities of peace from the viewpoint of human and spiritual considerations. Moreover, it is practically impossible to bring the world politically under one system or under one ideology. History has abundantly proved this to be so. The whole world, however, can be one on a spiritual basis and it is *only* on this basis that it can be one.

God is one and He is in every one of us. This is a universal truth. The greater the devotion towards God, the more we find we are nearer one another. The more we forget Him, the more do we begin to draw away from one another, whether as people or as nations. The modern trend generally is to ignore the Lord and try to pursue happiness through worldly possessions and achievements. The more we run in this direction, the more unhappy and frustrated do we become.

We can only achieve happiness, even while living in this world, through devotion and love of the Lord. For example, a child holding his father's hand goes to a fair, and everything he sees is of great amusement and joy to him. He thinks, perhaps, he is getting all this pleasure by what he sees in the fair. However, if by chance he loses his father's grip and is lost in the crowd, although the whole fair is still there, he begins to cry, and nothing attracts him any more. Then he realizes that this fair was a source of enjoyment only while he was holding his father's hand. Our Father is the Lord only. When we are in touch with Him, this whole world is a source of joy for us.

Excerpts from letters written to Diwan Daryai Lal from overseas satsangis during Maharaj Ji's visit to U.S.A. June 21, 1964

He is the most beautiful, kind and loving Jewel. I had the pleasure of seeing this great saint in human form for four days and nights, also had a dinner with him. What a gift, how you must have missed him at Dera!

We just loved and adored him, and forgot how you missed him. Once he is in your presence, you don't want to leave him.

***

. . . I am indeed so sorry that Maharaj Ji— your most precious, adorable, dearest, lovable sweetheart, and sweetest darling—is not physically with you, but his loving heart beats for all of us here and with you all there.

Dear brother Daryai Lal, your plea to hear about darling Maharaj Ji filled this heart with love

and gratitude. To be able to write about Maharaj Ji
reminds one of a poem written to describe a lover's
love for his beloved. . . . May I write it, as it is a
great reminder to me of how you must feel in your
heart for Maharaj Ji.

> The love you have aroused in me
>   Robs me of reason,
> Prevents me from eating and sleeping,
>   Cuts me off from my friends,
> Makes glory seem undesirable and victory worthless,
>   Unless it pleases Thee.
> It is an all-encompassing love
>   That drives me to the verge of frenzy.
> My heart is aflame, my blood burns.

May his all-encompassing lovableness fill all
your hearts with such endearment, and unite you to
his tenderness and his glory forever and ever!

My deepest gratitude to you for reminding me
of the beloved's love and of his lovable lovers.

———

The Last Chapter

When Maharaj Ji returned from Delhi after satsang in March 1990, we observed that he was not interested in whatever was happening around him, although he was taking care of everything in the normal routine. I could not help asking him what the matter was. He replied, "Nothing interests me and nothing holds me here. My work is done." These words came as a rude shock to me. Filled with dread, my fear provoked me to say, "The Great Master left this world at the age of 90. You are only 73."

While at Delhi he had felt pain in his heart. After coming to the Dera, his E.C.G. was taken, and the doctor advised him to reduce his daily activities and take more rest. The doctor also prescribed some medicine to be taken regularly. The days passed by, but the fear of what he had said continued to rankle in the heart. He appeared to be in good health throughout the week and attended to his normal routine, except that one day he complained of being breathless during his evening walk and therefore stopped it. The May bhandara was approaching and he got busy with his regular activities. On the bhandara day, after satsang, he said he was feeling pain, off and on, in the heart region since the morning. We tried to persuade him that he should immediately show himself to the doctor and take rest. He directed us not to mention anything to anyone. "There is nothing to worry," he said, "I have already talked to Dr. Joshi, who will take my E.C.G. in the evening."

In spite of the pain, he went to the langar in the hottest part of the day to bless the food, and from there to the seva. He gave interviews and went through all that he normally did. In the early evening an E.C.G. was taken by Dr. Joshi, but it was normal. After that he again continued with his regular routine, and went to see Beji (his mother), although the pain continued. After staying with Beji till about 7.45 p.m., he did not wait to take his food with the family, but went to his bedroom to rest, and had his meal by himself.

Next morning, that is on the 28th May, Dr. Joshi again took his E.C.G., which showed slight changes. The result of the blood test, however, indicated that he was suffering from infraction in the heart. Consequently, at the insistence of the doctors and the executive committee, the initiation programme was cancelled.

Maharaj Ji's words continued to haunt my mind and I felt a deep-rooted fear. We waited for some word from him to call us for darshan. To our good fortune, a message came in the evening that he was calling us. We had been worried the whole day and this message carried a ray of hope that he must be feeling better. So Louise, Mrs. Bharat Ram and I went to see him. Dr. Joshi was there and requested us to refrain from making any conversation. We were very happy to have his darshan and felt greatly relieved when he said that he was feeling better. We sat for about ten minutes, and left the room thinking that a few days' bed rest would cure him and again he would continue with his normal routine.

Little did we realize that he had decided to leave this world, and that this was just an excuse he had found to divert us.

The next day, on the 29th, the three of us, along with my husband, were called in the morning at about 10.30 a.m. He had developed some congestion in the chest and had slight difficulty in talking, although he said he was better.

He was so gracious, that in spite of his deteriorating health, he sent for us in the evening, and gave some instructions to my husband. We were there for a few minutes and were extremely grateful for his grace.

On the morning of Wednesday, May 30th, Huzur Maharaj Ji called the Dera Secretary, Shri S. L. Sondhi, and some other senior satsangis. He had asked all doctors (except Dr. Joshi), nurses and members of the family to leave the room. What the Master then said came as a terrible shock to all of them. He dictated his will to the Secretary, appointing Sardar Gurinder Singh Dhillon, son of Sardar Gurmukh Singh Dhillon of Moga, as his spiritual successor, entrusting him with the power and authority to give satsangs, initiate seekers, and appointed him as the Patron of the Radha Soami Satsang Beas Society and Maharaj Jagat Singh Medical Relief Society Beas.

After the will was completed, putting on his reading glasses, Maharaj Ji went through it carefully. It was also read out to all the witnesses.

While dictating the will, Huzur Maharaj Ji's

voice, though slightly weak, was clear and firm, and when he signed it his face was shining, radiant. The document was then signed by witnesses—Shri S. L. Sondhi, Dr. P. S. Joshi, S. Sewa Singh and Shri V. K. Sethi. As per Huzur's instructions, S. Sohan Singh Bhandari also signed as Headman (Sarpanch) of the village over the stamp of his office.

A little later Maharaj Ji called Shri S. L.. Sondhi and one of the witnesses to his room and gave them instructions about making xerox copies of the will and keeping the original in the Dera safe. The execution of the will gave a shattering blow to all present. But, seeing their moist eyes and expressions full of agony, Huzur said, "Sondhi Sahib, don't worry, I'll be all right." They walked down, a bit relieved, to follow his directions about the safe-keeping of the document.

On the 31st early morning, Maharaj Ji told Dr. Joshi, who was attending on him, "This body is no longer fit for seva, so what is the point of keeping it?" Dr. Joshi protested and said that this state of health might be a temporary phase, that he should be able to recover, and in course of time, function normally. He further reminded him of his promise that he would be all right. Maharaj Ji replied, "Everything is happening according to the will of the Lord."

Later that morning, we were again called at about the same time. He had asked the doctors to remove the oxygen. The unusual glow on his face was such that nobody could think he was ill. His voice was a little weak, though clear. He was

giving advice to his children to live in love and
harmony. He spoke a few words to the four of us
and gave instructions to my husband and to Louise.
My mind, however, was completely blank with grief.
We bowed our heads and came out, little realizing
that this was the last physical darshan that we would
have of our beloved Master.

On the morning of June 1st we were told that
a heart specialist had come from Delhi, and Maharaj
Ji was being examined by her. So we waited in our
room, but my husband went to Maharaj Ji's house
to inquire about his health. At 11.30 a.m. he came
and said that Maharaj Ji's condition was critical. We
then went with him to the house, thinking we would
wait there. But on reaching the drawing room, we
heard the dreaded news that our beloved Master had
shed his mortal coil and merged back into the
Shabd. Though he is always with us, the tremendous
loss of his physical presence was a great shock to
all of us.

The news of his departure spread like wildfire
all over the Dera, India and abroad. To the satsangis
it was a bolt from the blue, stunning and totally
unbelievable. Everyone wanted confirmation. People
thought some cruel joke had been played upon them.
Only five days ago he had delivered the monthly
satsang. But alas, the news was correct. Everyone
inquired, "How could it have happened?" Such was
His will.

From that moment onwards, for satsangis, all
roads led to Beas. Everyone wanted to rush there,
by whatever means available, to have a last glimpse

of their beloved Satguru. To all of them, he had been a friend, a teacher, a father, a Satguru, and in fact, the Lord himself. He was the focal point of life in this world and the only hope for the life beyond. They wanted to reach Beas in time to have the last 'darshan' of their Master's physical form.

His mortal frame was lying in state for darshan at the satsang compound, on a specially prepared reclining dais in front of the place from where he had delivered satsangs for the last several decades, in all his majesty and glory. Millions were rushing to the Dera. The traffic on the Grand Trunk road was blocked for 15 km. from all directions leading to Beas. The road between the railway station and the Dera was absolutely jammed by trucks, trolleys, vans, cars, taxis, and every imaginable mode of transport. People had to abandon their vehicles on the road and in the fields and join the tremendous crowd inching its way to Dera. Everyone was in a hurry. Nobody thought of anything else. No one heard anyone else. There was an ocean of humanity on the move. Still, only a fraction reached the place in time: the short distance from Beas to Dera took the hurrying crowds 5 hours at this agonizingly slow pace. Even the State Government dignitaries and police officials were held up on the way, and they were unable to pay their last homage. The best estimates of the crowds were from 10 to 12 lakhs (1,000,000 to 1,200,000).

On June 2nd, in the early hours of the morning, people filed past the bier in the satsang compound. There he was, beautiful and serene as ever, radiating the familiar divine glow, the magnificent white beard, and the same benign expression of tranquillity on his face, which had won the hearts of friends and foes alike.

Some of the family members, sorrow written deeply on their faces, were sitting around the bier. Lakhs and lakhs filed past, having his last darshan, quietly and peacefully, perfectly disciplined, just as he would have liked them to be.

At 8.00 a.m. sharp, the bier was taken to the cremation ground, through the Dera, every brick of which had been laid under his and his predecessors' loving guidance. On both sides of the road, thousands stood with folded hands, sobbing. There were touching scenes all around. Many cried aloud and others silently shed tears. When the procession reached the cremation ground, a huge crowd had already gathered there.

The body was placed on the carefully arranged pyre. The last rites were performed by the successor and Maharaj Ji's two sons.

As the pyre was lit, a huge sob arose from all those present. It was the end, and the start of a new beginning. The light had merged, but another had been lit.

In his passing away, many would think that a vacuum had been created, a void that could never be filled, that the Dera had lost its prime mover, satsang had lost its mentor, the disciples all over the world had become orphans. But this is not so. He had made his will, appointing a successor. The light is in him now. He has been given all the powers, spiritual and temporal. He who believed in perfection, has left a perfect Master to convey his message of love for the Lord and His creation, and to lead all souls yearning to meet Him, to the path of union with the Lord.

None of us would ever have imagined that the transition from Huzur Maharaj Ji to the present Master could be so smooth. This is due to Huzur Maharaj Ji's grace. The love that his disciples felt for him gave them the strength and spiritual maturity to accept His will and to receive and welcome His successor into their hearts. The present Master has taken on the work of the Dera from the point where his Master left it. All perfect Masters come from the same source and all have the same powers.

On June 10th the successor appeared before the sangat on the dais for the first time.

It was the day when the traditional 'Dastarbandi' ceremony, the formal inauguration, took place. Babaji's shawl and Maharaj Ji's turban were presented to him by Maharaj Ji's brother, Capt. P.S. Grewal.

The present Master removed his own turban and tied Maharaj Ji's turban on his head, and wrapped Babaji's shawl around his shoulders. The sangat, so far in anguish, was consoled by the sight of the present Master, and his loving countenance was a comfort to every heart. After bowing to the sangat, he spoke a few words which were filled with love and humility. His heart was full and he had to pause after practically every sentence. The sangat could feel the vibrations of love all through the speech, for every word carried and conveyed much more than its literal meaning.

Maharaj Ji's Will

I, S. Charan Singh Grewal s/o S. Harbans Singh Grewal, aged 74 years am making this Will in regard to the spiritual affairs of the Society, Radha Soami Satsang Beas while in full possession of my wits.

I am making this Will in accordance with the wishes of Hazur Maharaj Baba Sawan Singh Ji Maharaj and my predecessor. I have served the Sangat whole-heartedly to the best of my ability for nearly forty years. I have received in great measure the love, faith and esteem of the entire sangat, of sewadars and my staff members of which it would be difficult to find a parallel in this world. I am deeply grateful for their co-operation and support.

I appoint Sh. Gurinder Singh Dhillon S/o Sh. Gurmukh Singh Dhillon of Moga as my spiritual successor as ordered by Hazur Maharaj Baba Sawan Singh Ji Maharaj. He will be the Sant Satguru as well as the Patron of Radha Soami Satsang Beas and will have the authority of giving initiation (NAM). He will also be the Patron of Maharaj Jagat Singh Medical Relief Society.

I have made this Will in accordance with the wishes of Hazur Maharaj Baba Sawan Singh Ji Maharaj and I have every hope that my wishes as expressed in this will be duly honoured by the entire sangat, all my family members and members of the Society.

Witnessed by   Sd/-

1. Sewa Singh   4. P. S. Joshi   Charan Singh
2. S. L. Sondhi   DR. P. S. JOSHI
dated 30-5-90
at Dera Baba Jaimal Singh   3. Virendra Kumar Sethi

[In the left-hand margin]
    S.S. Bhandari
        30-5-90   Charan Singh
        Sarpanch
Gram Panchayat Dera Baba Jaimal Singh
        Zila Amritsar

———

I, S. Charan Singh Grewal s/o S Harbans Singh Grewal, aged 74 years am making this will in regard to the spiritual affairs of the Society, Radhasoami Satsang Beas which in full possession of my will.

I am making this will in accordance with the wishes of Hazur Maharaj Baba Sawan Singh Ji: history & my predecessor. I have served the Satsang whole-heartedly to the best of my ability for nearly forty years. I have received in great measure the love, faith and esteem of the entire satsangat, of Sewadars and my staff members of which it would be difficult to find a parallel in the world. I am deeply grateful for their Co-operation and support

I appoint Sh. Gurinder Singh Dhillon S/o Sh Gurmukh Singh Dhillon of Moga as my spiritual successor as ordered by Hazur Maharaj Baba Jawan Singh Ji Maharaj. He will be the Sant Satguru as will as the Patron of Radhasoami Satsang Beas and will have the authority of giving initiation (NAM). He will also be the Patron of Maharaj Jagat Singh Medical Relief Society.

I have made this will in accordance with the wishes of Hazur Maharaj Baba Sawan Singh Ji Maharaj and I have every hope that my wishes as expressed in this will be duly honoured by the entire sangat, all my family members and members of the society

Witnesses:

1. Daya Singh —
2. Sd. Sardar
dated 30-5-90
at Dera Baba Jaimal Singh

4. Joshi
DR. P.S. JOSHI

3. Virendra Kumar Sethi

A.S. Bhandari 30.5.70

ਸਰਪੰਚ
ਗਰਾਮ ਪੰਚਾਇਤ

Address by Shri S.L. Sondhi, Secretary
Radha Soami Satsang Beas
June 10, 1990

As the sangat is aware, we have assembled here this morning to witness the auspicious ceremony of "Dastarbandi" of the Successor of our late beloved Huzur Maharaj Ji. However, with the permission of the sangat, I should like to say a few words by way of my humble tribute to the greatness of Huzur Maharaj Ji.

The indisposition of Huzur Maharaj Ji, which eventually led to His sad demise, started on the morning of 27th May, the day on which He was to deliver the last of the series of bhandara satsangs. On medical grounds, He would have been advised not to undergo the exertion of doing the satsang. However, so great was His love for the sangat and His anxiety to avoid causing disappointment to the immensely large assemblage, that He gave the satsang, which was marked by the forceful manner in which it was delivered. Later in the day, His indisposition started taking a turn for the worse. The very best treatment that was provided was of no avail, and after a brief illness of five days He chose to go beyond life's gateway, merging in the Supreme Shabd, plunging the entire sangat into the depths of grief and sorrow.

Huzur Maharaj Ji was a perfect saint, sent into this world by the Lord for the liberation of souls. It is impossible for a mere mortal like me to make a realistic estimation of His great qualities. All that I

MAHARAJ GURINDER SINGH

can say is that with the great charm of His personality, His spiritual eminence, His towering wisdom and intelligence, the nobility and purity of His life, His simple style of living and His generosity and liberality, he had created a deep impression on the minds of satsangis and the general public alike. According to the tenets of Sant Mat, He earned His livelihood by scrupulously honest means, not accepting even a penny of the sangat. Nay, He spared a sizeable portion of His income for the seva of the sangat. We shall remember Him till the very end of our days for His high principles and lofty ideals.

Huzur Maharaj Ji's ministry as a Sant Satguru lasted for nearly forty years. He devoted Himself wholeheartedly to the task of promoting the cause of Sant Mat by frequent tours to almost all parts of India and several places in foreign countries, and by writing books on Sant Mat that have earned popularity, the like of which has rarely fallen to the lot of any author. In short, He did not spare Himself any pain for spreading the gospel of Sant Mat far and wide. It was His pet saying that the human frame should be put to the best possible use for the good of humanity. His achievement by way of liberation of souls has no parallel, for He initiated nearly twelve lakhs of persons and bestowed on them the privilege of entry into Sach Khand. He guided very successfully the destiny of the institution of which He was the chief, and raised it to the status of a highly esteemed spiritual centre of the world. It was through His untiring efforts that Radha Soami Mat today is respected by one and all, and

its followers, spread in nearly fifty countries of the world, are held in high esteem for their righteous living, character, conduct and their love and compassion for their fellow beings.

Huzur Maharaj Ji's achievements on the worldly plane are no less glorious. He started the practice of holding free eye camps, which have now become an annual feature of the activities of the Dera. More than five thousand patients are treated free of all cost at these camps every year. He established a big and beautiful hospital where all and sundry without any distinction of caste, colour and creed, particularly those belonging to rural areas, are treated free of charge. There cannot possibly be any hospital anywhere in the world to hold a candle to this hospital.

Alas, the Lord chose to call the Divine Soul back to His Eternal Home, after He had done His duty towards the marked souls on this earth.

Fortunately for us, Huzur Maharaj Ji has left a will to ensure continuance of the line of Gurus in the Dera. By His will, executed on 30th May, 1990 and witnessed by four of His disciples, he appointed Shri Gurinder Singh Dhillon, son of Shri Gurmukh Singh Dhillon, as His Successor. His will is going to be read out to the sangat, first in English and then in Punjabi. It was Huzur's last wish that His Successor should be given the same love and esteem which His sangat had for Him. It is made clear in the will that His Successor will not only be the Sant Satguru after Him, but will also have the authority and privilege of bestowing initiation,

besides being Patron of the Satsang Society and the Medical Relief Society. Accordingly, the administration of the affairs of the Dera, the performance of spiritual duties and promotion of the welfare of the sangat, all of which were taken care of by Huzur Maharaj Ji, have been entrusted to the Successor. It, therefore, behoves us to carry out the wishes of Huzur Maharaj Ji, and look upon the Successor as His embodiment, i.e., Word made flesh.

> *[The ceremony of Dastarbandi was then gone through. Capt. P.S. Grewal presented the turban to our new Guru who, after wearing it, took His seat on the "asan" (mat) of Baba Jaimal Singh Ji Maharaj]*

————

Maharaj Gurinder Singh Ji's Inaugural Address June 10, 1990

I have no words to express the deep anguish and sorrow caused to all of us by Huzur Maharaj Ji's departure from this earthly plane. He chose to make a minor illness an excuse for leaving us, to merge back into the Source of Love and Light from which he came, thus casting a shadow of gloom over the entire world. Medically, he could have recovered from the illness; but, having completed the Divine Mission assigned to him, he chose to cast off the mortal coil. This servant is unable to say much to the sangat at this time except that, in obedience to the orders of the Great Master and my beloved Satguru Maharaj Ji, I have come to present myself in your service.

I had come to the Dera on leave for a month and a half to attend to some personal affairs and to spend as much time as possible at the feet of Huzur Maharaj Ji. In common with the sangat, I could never imagine that he would leave us so suddenly, nor even in my dreams could I ever think that the burden of such a heavy responsibility would be thrown on my shoulders by Huzur Maharaj Ji. I find myself quite lacking and do not consider myself worthy of the seva assigned to me, for I am but a particle of dust at the feet of the sangat. When I look to my shortcomings, I wonder how I shall be able to shoulder the heavy responsibility of serving the sangat. I am not capable of doing anything without the grace of Huzur Maharaj Ji. It is this servant's humble understanding that whatever seva has been assigned to me by Huzur Maharaj Ji, he will undertake the responsibility, using me as his instrument.

The events have left me in a daze and I feel quite lost, but have no option save to carry out the orders of my Satguru. I am entering upon the performance of my duties in the hope and with the confidence that the sangat, treating me as their humble servant, will give their fullest cooperation and shower on me just a little bit from the vast ocean of love that they have for Huzur Maharaj Ji. With these words I dedicate myself to the service of the sangat.

Let us all join in supplication to Babaji Maharaj and Huzur Maharaj Ji that in this hour of our grief they may continue, as heretofore, to shower their grace on the sangat. Maharaj Ji had always been impressing upon us, during the forty years of his ministry, that there can be no salvation without the practice of Nam, and that this method of Surat-Shabd Yoga is the only means of attaining God-realization. All of us should, with full faith in the noble and lofty teachings of Huzur Maharaj Ji, and drawing inspiration from the ideal established by him during his lifetime through his own personal example, try to live the life of a good satsangi and continue to attend to meditation with love and devotion.

The sangat came from distant places, in very large numbers, for Huzur's last darshan. I notice that even today a huge number of devotees are present here, many coming from far-off places in India and abroad. The sangat must have undergone great suffering and hardship in this scorching heat, and there might have been several lapses in our arrangements, for which we beg to be forgiven by the sangat.

We are deeply grateful to you for coming and joining us in paying homage to Huzur Maharaj Ji, and for giving me an opportunity to meet you.

RADHA SOAMI

INDEX

A

Administration, Dera, 3-9, 28, 50, 86, 129, 147
Agra, 71, 154, 166-75, 186, 205
Ahluwalia, Mr., 8, 30, 78-79, 120-21, 232
Akbar, Emperor, 185-87
American satsangis, 189, 198, 260, 264, 266-67, 272-74.
    See also Charan Singh Ji Maharaj
Army depot, 117-18, 199, 240-241
Attitude of mind, 196

B

Babaji. *See* Jaimal Singh Ji Maharaj
Bachint Singh, Sardar, 35-36, 88-89
Bahota (Himachal), 114, 191
Balsarai school, 142, 151
Balwant Singh, Sardar, 6
Bangalore, 195
Banyan tree, 38
Beji (Maharaj Ji's mother), 11, 15, 41-42, 49, 55, 57-58,
    73-74, 136, 138, 176-78, 227, 241-42, 277
Berg, Col., 271
Bhagat Singh, Sardar 36, 92, 152
Birthdays of saints, 221-22. *See also* Charan Singh Ji Maharaj
Birth and death, 156, 221

C

Calcutta, 248-49
Caste or creed, 101, 142, 175-78. *See also* Harijans
Ceremonies and rituals, 59, 103, 163-66, 206-08, 221, 238

Charan Singh Ji Maharaj (*cont.*)
    relations (*cont.*)
        children, 55, 58-59, 178, 201, 236
        father, 10, 11-14, 34-35, 41, 55-57, 59-60, 61,
            139-47, 227
        father-in-law, 236-38, 248-50
        grandfather. *See above,* Great Master; *see also*
            Sawan Singh Ji Maharaj
        grandmother, 65-69
        mother (Beji), 11, 15, 41-42, 49, 55, 57-58, 73-74,
            136, 138, 176-78, 227, 241-42, 277
        sisters, 42, 49, 58, 143
        wife (Harjit), 55, 58, 135-36, 138, 143, 176, 178,
            201, 236
    reminiscences, 241-43
    Russia, trip, 206-08
    Sardar Bahadur Ji, relationship with, 44, 48-50, 61-62,
        74-75. *See also* Jagat Singh Ji Maharaj
    salad incident (England), 183-84
    sangat's love for, 118-20
    satsangs of, 226-27, 268-69
    sayings, 178-81
    sevadars, 160-63
    sixty days' meditation, 222-23
    smallpox, 135-37
    successor, Maharaj Ji's, 278, 282-93
    successorship
        Ahluwalia's acceptance, 30
        attempted escape from Dera, 9, 20-21, 137
        difficulties after installation, 3-9, 28-31
        father's persuasion, 138
        first learned, 13-16
        hesitation, 137-39
        Hillman car, 11
        inauguration, 62-65, 123-24, 138
        initial reaction, 22-28
        Prof. Jagmohan Lal's realization, 29

Muslims, 139-42, 175-78. *See also* Partition

N

Nam, 156-57, 171, 221-22, 284, 293. *See also* Initiation
Nanak, Guru, 238

P

Pahwa, Dr. J. M., 98-99
Parshad, 100-01, 108-09
Partition, 4, 5, 51, 107, 131, 139, 149, 177, 199
Pilgrimage places, 108
Politics, 155, 157-60. *See also* Charan Singh Ji Maharaj
Poona, 204
Prejudices 6, 139, 175-78. *See also* Satsangi/non-satsangi
Priests, 208

R

Rajasthan, 202
Rali, Bibi (Bhua Ji), 12-13, 15, 20, 44, 66, 72, 83, 87,
    133-34, 136, 173, 177, 222-23, 270
Rao Sahib, 35, 67, 236-38, 248-49
Relationships, 32, 197, 237
Religion, 207-08
Rituals and ceremonies, 59, 103, 164-66, 206, 207-08, 221, 238
Rukko, Bibi, 89, 91, 242-43
Russia, Maharaj Ji's visit (1979), 206-07

S

Sadhu on horseback incident, 74-75
Saigon, 193
Sanders, Col., 183
Sangli, His Highness of, 204
Sar Bachan, 91, 170, 225

Information and Books
are available from

The Secretary
Radha Soami Satsang Beas
P.O. Dera Baba Jaimal Singh 143 204
District Amritsar, Punjab, India

AFGHANISTAN
Mr. Manak Singh, c/o Manaco, P.O. Box 3163, Kabul

AUSTRALIA
Mrs. Janet Bland, P.O. Box 3, Oaklands Park, South Australia 5046

AUSTRIA
Mr. Hansjorg Hammerer, Sezenweingasse 10, A-5020 Salzburg

BARBADOS
Mr. Bhagwandas Kessaram, c/o Kiddies Corner, Swan Street,
    Bridgetown

BRAZIL
Inquiries in Portuguese may be addressed to the Representative listed
    under Portugal

CANADA
Dr. J. Khanna, 5550 McMaster Rd., Vancouver, B.C., V6T IJ8
Dr. Peter Grayson, 177 Division St., Kingsville, Ontario, N9Y IRI

CYPRUS
Mr. Hercules Achilleos, Kyriakou Matsi 18, Pallouriotissa-T.K. 9077,
    Nicosia

CZECHOSLOVAKIA
Mr. Vladimir Skalsky, Uralska 9, CS-160 00 Prague 6

DENMARK
Ms. Inge Gregersen, Askevenget-15, 2830 Virum

DUBAI
Mr. Chander Bhatia, Shabnam Trading Corp., P.O. Box 2296

ECUADOR
Dr. Gonzalo Vargas Noeriega, Calle Montalvo #200, Oficina 201,
    P.O. Box 17-01-2666, Quito

FRANCE
Count Pierre de Proyart, 7 Quai Voltaire, 75007 Paris

GERMANY
Mr. Rudolf Walberg, P.O. Box 1544, D-6232 Bad Soden/Taunus

GHANA
Mr. J.O.K. Sekyi, P.O. Box 4615, Accra

GIBRALTAR
Mr. Sunder Mahtani, Radha Soami Satsang Beas, 401 Ocean Heights

GREECE
Dr. Constantine Siopoulos, Thrakis 7, 145 61 Kifissia

GUYANA
Mrs. Rajni B. Manglani, c/o Bhagwan's Store, 18 Water Street, Georgetown

HAITI
Mr. Sean Finnegan, P.O. Box 2314, Port-au-Prince

HOLLAND
Mr. Jacob Hofstra, Geulwijk 6, 3831 LM Leusden

HONG KONG
Mr. S.G. Dasani, T.S.T., P.O. Box 96567, Kowloon
Mrs. Cami Moss, Viewpoint, 7 Bowen Road, Block A,
    Ground floor No. 1

INDONESIA
Mr. G.L. Nanwani, Yayasan Radha Soami Satsang Beas, J.L. Kelinci Raya No. 32 A, Jakarta-Pusat
Mr. Tarachand Chotrani, 51 Dji, Bubutan, P.O. Box 144, Surabaya

ISRAEL
Mrs. H. Mandelbaum, P.O. Box 2815, Tel Aviv - 61000

ITALY
Mr. Ted Goodman, Via Garigliano 27, Rome 00198

JAPAN
Mr. L.H. Parwani, Radha Soami Satsang Beas, 2-18 Nakajimadori, 1-Chome, Aotani, Fukiai-Ku, Kobe - 651

KENYA
Mr. Surinder Singh Ghir, P.O. Box 39993, Nairobi

KUWAIT
Mr. & Mrs. Ghassan Alghanem, P.O. Box 25549, 13116 Safat

Local Addresses

LIBERIA
Mr. Krishin Vaswani, Vaan-Ahn Enterprises Ltd., P.O. Box 507, Monrovia

MALAYSIA
Dr. Narjit Dhaliwal, Kampulan Perubatan SMP, No. 18, Lorong Sempadan, Jalan 16/7, P.O. Box 81, 40000 Shah Alam

MASCARENE ISLANDS
Mr. D.S. Sumboo, 9 Bis Harris Street, Port Louis, Mauritius

MEXICO
Mr. Jorge Angel Santana, Cameta 2821, Jardines Del Bosque, Guadalajara, Jalisco

NEW ZEALAND
Mr. Tony Waddicor, P.O. Box 5331, Wellesley St. P.O., Auckland 1

NIGERIA
Mr. N.N. Balani, GPO Box 10407, Marina, Lagos

PHILIPPINES
Mr. Kay Sham, P.O. Box 2346 MCC, Makati, Metro, Manila

PORTUGAL
Mr. Alberto C. Ferreira, Apartado 5279, 1707 Lisbon CODEX

SINGAPORE
Mr. Bhojraj T. Mirwani, 19 Amber Road, Singapore 1543

SOUTH AFRICA
Mr. Sam Busa, P.O. Box 41355, Craighall, Transvaal 2024
Mr. R. Atwell, P.O. Box 5702, Durban 4000

SPAIN
Mr. H.W. Balani, Balani's International, P.O. Box 486, Malaga

SRILANKA
Mr. D.H. Jiwat, Geekay Ltd., 33 Bankshall Street, Colombo - 11

SWEDEN
Mr. Lennart Zachen, Liebackskroken, 10A, 2tr, S-256 58, Helsingborg

SWITZERLAND
Mr. Olivier de Coulon, Rue de Centre, CH-1131, Tolochenaz

TAIWAN
Mr. L.T. Nanwani, Room No.508 Chou Woo House, 57 Tun Hwa Road, Taipei

Local Addresses

TANZANIA

Mr. D.N. Pandit, K. Lands Limited, P.O. Box 1963, Dar-es-Salaam

THAILAND

Mr. Harmahinder Singh Sethi, Sawan Textiles Ltd., 154 Serm Sin Kha, Sampheng, Bangkok - 10100

TRINIDAD

Mr. Thakurdas Chatlani, 2A Gittins Avenue, Maraval

UGANDA

Mr. Sylvester Kakooza, P.O. Box 31381, Kampala

U.K.

Mrs. F.E. Wood, Willow Cottage, Worple Road, Leatherhead, Surrey, K.T. 22 8HG

U.S.A.

Mr. Roland G. de Vries, 10901 Mill Springs Drive, Nevada City, Calif. 95959

Dr. Gene Ivash, 4701 Shadow Lane, Austin, Texas 78731

Mr. Roy E. Ricks, 651 Davis Street, Melrose Park, Ill. 60160

Mr. Henry F. Weekley, 2121 N. Ocean Blvd., Apt. 1108E, Boca Raton, Fla. 33431

VENEZUELA

Mr. Leopoldo Luks, Ave. Maracay, Urb. Las Palmas, Qta. Luksenburg, Caracas

YUGOSLAVIA

Mr. Marko Bedina, Brezje Pri Trzicu 68, 64290 Trzic

ZIMBABWE

Mrs. B. Schwerzel, 12 Churchill Drive, P.O. Marlborough-Harare

FOR OTHER FOREIGN ORDERS WRITE TO:

Mr. Krishin Babani, Buona Casa Bldg., 2nd Floor, Sir P.M. Road, Fort, Bombay - 400 001, India

Addresses changed since this book was printed:

FOR
UK BOOK INFORMATION
AND ENQUIRIES
PLEASE RING
081 310 3343

Books on this Science

Soami Ji Maharaj
1. *Sar Bachan*

Baba Jaimal Singh
2. *Spiritual Letters* (to Huzur Maharaj Sawan Singh: 1896-1903)

Huzur Maharaj Sawan Singh
3. *The Dawn of Light* (letters: 1911-1934)
4. *Discourses on Sant Mat*
5. *Philosophy of the Masters (Gurmat Sidhant)*, 5 vols. (an encyclopedia on the teachings of the saints)
6. *Philosophy of the Masters* (abridged)
7. *My Submission* (introduction to *Philosophy of the Masters*)
8. *Spiritual Gems* (letters: 1919-1948)
9. *Tales of the Mystic East* (as narrated in satsangs)

Sardar Bahadur Maharaj Jagat Singh
10. *The Science of the Soul* (discourses and letters: 1948-1951)

Maharaj Charan Singh
11. *Die to Live* (answers to questions on meditation)
12. *Teachings of the Saints* (first chapter of *Die to Live*)
13. *Divine Light* (discourses and letters: 1959-1964)
14. *The Path* (first part of *Divine Light*)
15. *Light on Saint John*
16. *Light on Saint Matthew*
17. *Light on Sant Mat* (discourse and letters: 1952-1958)
18. *The Master Answers* (to audiences in America: 1964)
19. *Quest for Light* (letters: 1965-1971)
20. *Spiritual Discourses*
21. *Spiritual Heritage* (from tape-recorded talks)
22. *Thus Saith the Master* (to audiences in America: 1970)
23. *Truth Eternal* (a discourse)
24. *Way to God* (a discourse)

Books about the Masters

1. *Call of the Great Master*—Diwan Daryai Lal Kapur
2. *Heaven on Earth*—Diwan Daryai Lal Kapur
3. *The Living Master*—Katherine Wason
4. *Treasure beyond Measure*—Shanti Sethi
5. *With a Great Master in India*—Dr. Julian P. Johnson
6. *With the Three Masters*, 3 vols.—from the diary of Rai Sahib Munshi Ram

Books about Sant Mat in general

1. *The Holy Name, Mysticism in Judaism*—Miriam Bokser Caravella
2. *In Search of the Way*—Flora E. Wood
3. *The Inner Voice*—Colonel C.W. Sanders
4. *Kabir, the Great Mystic*—Isaac A. Ezekiel
5. *Liberation of the Soul*—J. Stanley White, Ph.D.
6. *Message Divine*—Shanti Sethi
7. *Mystic Bible*—Dr. Randolph Stone
8. *The Mystic Philosophy of Sant Mat*—Peter Fripp
9. *Mysticism, The Spiritual Path*, 2 vols.—Prof. Lekh Raj Puri
10. *The Path of the Masters*—Dr. Julian P. Johnson
11. *Radha Soami Teachings*—Prof. Lekh Raj Puri
12. *The Ringing Radiance*—Sir Colin Garbett
13. *Sant Mat and the Bible*—Narain Das
14. *Sarmad, Jewish Saint of India*—Isaac A. Ezekiel
15. *A Soul's Safari*—Netta Pfeifer
16. *Teachings of the Gurus*—Prof. Lekh Raj Puri
17. *Yoga and the Bible*—Joseph Leeming

Mystics of the East Series

1. *Bulleh Shah*—J.R. Puri and T.R. Shangari
2. *Dadu, the Compassionate Mystic*—K.N. Upadhyaya, Ph.D.
3. *Dariya Sahib, Saint of Bihar*—K.N. Upadhyaya, Ph.D.
4. *Guru Nanak, His Mystic Teachings*—J.R. Puri
5. *Guru Ravidas, Life and Teachings*—K.N. Upadhyaya, Ph.D.
6. *Kabir, the Weaver of God's Name*—V.K. Sethi
7. *Mira, the Divine Lover*—V.K. Sethi
8. *Saint Namdev, His Life and Teachings*—J.R. Puri and V.K. Sethi
9. *Saint Paltu*—Isaac A. Ezekiel
10. *Tukaram, Saint of Maharashtra*—C. Rajwade
11. *Tulsi Sahib, Saint of Hathras*—J.R. Puri and V.K. Sethi